C000118617

THE AMBASSADOR
Growing Community Leaders

Rachel Nyambura Walton

10-10-10
Publishing

THE AMBASSADOR: Growing Community Leaders
www.communityambassador.co.uk
Copyright © 2021 Rachel Nyambura Walton

ISBN: 979-8749976816

All rights reserved. No portion of this book may be reproduced mechanically, electronically, or by any other means, including photocopying, without permission of the publisher or author except in the case of brief quotations embodied in critical articles and reviews. It is illegal to copy this book, post it to a website, or distribute it by any other means without permission from the publisher or author.

References to internet websites (URLs) were accurate at the time of writing. Authors and the publishers are not responsible for URLs that may have expired or changed since the manuscript was prepared.

Limits of Liability and Disclaimer of Warranty
The author and publisher shall not be liable for your misuse of the enclosed material. This book is strictly for informational and educational purposes only.

Warning – Disclaimer
The purpose of this book is to educate and entertain. The author and/or publisher do not guarantee that anyone following these techniques, suggestions, tips, ideas, or strategies will become successful. The author and/or publisher shall have neither liability nor responsibility to anyone with respect to any loss or damage caused, or alleged to be caused, directly or indirectly by the information contained in this book.

Publisher
10-10-10 Publishing
Markham, ON Canada

Printed in Canada and the United States of America

Table of Contents

My thanks to Nigel, David, Jacqui, Rose, Kate,
and all the Community Ambassadors, Advisory Group, Essex Community
Foundation, National Lottery 'Awards for All' and Community Fund.

Thanks also to Damaris, Siddika, Munevver, Kanyinsola,
Kumaiza, Khainjyah, Hasina, Pascale, Jessy, Dilek, Jemal, Fawzea,
Grace, and Jahanara

Praise for *The Ambassador*

This book identifies the importance of everyone working together. For some communities, it has been difficult to develop strong links between them and the organisations that should be there to protect and help them, because of a mutual lack of trust and understanding. Empowering women from within these communities and giving them skills to help each other and to link with helping agencies is an inspirational way forward.

Kate Evans
Former Stop the Traffik Modern Slavery Community Coordinator,
Safer Colchester Partnership Hub Team

This book provides a vivid account of Rachel Walton's exciting and inspiring journey of developing community projects through AFiUK. Through its pages it is possible to find a perfect example of a vocation for social justice that uses creativity, determination, planning and kindness in order to reach diverse communities across Essex.

Dr Carlos Gigoux
Deputy Director, Centre Migration Studies, Department of Sociology,
University of Essex

"The Ambassador - Growing Community Leaders" is a positive invitation to grow more leaders and understand the tools needed to grow capacity, including using the power of the network, storytelling, coaching and, most importantly, creating positive role models of which you are one yourself!

Steve Mostyn
Associate Fellow, Saïd Business School, University of Oxford

This book illustrates how we can all work collectively in our communities, by bringing things to light step by step, in an inclusive learning journey for all, through the power of networking, dialogue, joint problem-solving and connecting to our new heart-centred values in a society that enables all to thrive.

The journey, documented in earnest detail throughout this book, is a great inspiration to groups, and communities that seek to empower themselves in a post pandemic world of transformation and the power of the collective for a worthwhile life for each and every person. We all count. We can learn how to take our power back. And this book beautifully demonstrates how we can do this in a collective and collaborative way to truly make an impact.

An inspirational and honest account of how, when individuals and groups organise themselves in a way that makes sense to themselves, each can go forward with a mission that includes the core values of empowerment, self-development and reaching greater levels of potential.

Alex Klokkaris
Personal Development Consultant and owner of
Changing Lifecourse Training and Coaching

Thank you for sharing the very detailed journey you have undertaken on behalf of the community to which you volunteer your passion, enthusiasm and energy so freely. Since I first met you, I have been impressed by the commitment you have shown to ensure that everyone gets an equal opportunity to participate. I know the personal set-backs and disappointments you have experienced to acquire premises, funding and a whole host of other support needs to get where you are now. You don't give up, or in, which is admirable, and I am very proud of the work we have done together over the years. You always get my vote.

Well done to all that have contributed with you on this journey, and long may it continue.

Tracy Rudling
CEO C360

The title of this book is also a description of the writer, Rachel Walton, because really and truly she is an Ambassador for women's rights and development of the African community in the UK. And, in her own words, she is a people developer, growing leaders at every turn. This book is both a biography (of sorts) of her work, but also will serve as a guide for community developers across the UK and beyond. An amazing read from an amazing leader!

Kevin Korgba
John Maxwell Certified Leadership Trainer & Coach,
CEO L.E.A.D Global

This is a complete essay and book about how to run a charity organisation. It has vision, rules of engagement, standards of operations and the passion that is required to be part of such big and altruistic endeavour. Rachel's background as a missionary, and her love and care for people is evidenced in every page of the book. There is a clear understanding of the issues and even clearer path to solution, concentrating on the positive nature of the people afflicted and those, who want to help.

The inclusion and empowerment of the women in the community, and her plan to accommodate and cultural or linguistic difficulties, have been admirable and well thought out. The idea of bringing policy makers and those who want to help into a room to thrash out the issues and provide solutions shows that Rachel understands the importance of communication.

What I am also particularly happy about is the "growing leaders" and the "servant and transformational" approach to people development, and how people are developed so that they repeat the process, because then we have an organisation of servant leaders. I was fortunate enough to be a beneficiary of the numerous leadership and skills training from AFiUK CIC and the impact will be far reaching.

This is a compulsory read for anyone interested in the development of communities, and the notes from people associated with Rachel and have benefited from her selfless service is testimony to her character and delivery of excellence.

Onche Godwin Daudu
Director, IsedaleWa CIC, Community Ambassador of AFiUK. CIC

Rachel writes from lived experience. She writes from a place of informed compassion and a desire to create positive change. This book is a road map which anyone interested in creating empowering change within community can use.

Maria Wilby
Director, Colchester Refugee Action (CIC)

The ability to learn is the most important quality a leader can have."
(Padmasree Warrior, CEO & Founder, Fable). This is evident in Rachel's vision
and in the work of projects described in this book. It is evident by reading
about Rachel's and the UK(AFiUK) journey, that a legacy is been created that
inspires women and young girls to learn more, do more and become more.
This book advocates that leadership is strongest when it comes from our
community.

Jeannie Gordon QN & Debbi Barnes
The Ministry of Parenting CIC

Rachel, thank you for sharing this book with me. It was really interesting;
I don't think I have read anything quite like it for a number of reasons, all
related to culture, both yours and others'.

The book is a manual for 'mutual aid' — people in communities helping
each other, raising each other up so that they can help their community as a
whole, and give their communities a voice.

You have a clear philosophy which is all about growing people's potential.

You help people to value their identity, their ways of living and their
communities' strengths.

I think also, though, that this will be really valuable for everyone engaging
in mutual aid, whatever their reason for coming together. Your book is
practical, open and honest about your experiences and your challenges. You
are positive throughout, and the reader can see how you have approached
problems, the importance of a solid vision, why you should involve statutory
organisations, and the need to safeguard and nurture everyone involved. Your
quotes and statements are the evidence base that shows the reader how
successful you have been.

Sharon Rodie
Suffolk and North East Essex Integrated Care System,
Independent Social Work Consultant

How do you measure a self-belief that translates into a drive and fire that propels a project like this? Over the moments, weeks and now years that Rachel and I dreamt to be that hand that continued holding other migrant families and walking along with them until they and their children were securely attached to our adopted homeland, our actions and collaboration with others are starting to emerge as this organism that is reflecting not only a community's need for belonging, but that the community can itself find a space and create it into a safe and beautiful organic space that can accommodate all who need guidance, safety and belonging. AFiUK was born to provide a safety net for African migrant families, but we now welcome, include and are able to meet third culture families from various Asian regions, some Europeans and all regions of Africa. Read this book and catch a glimpse of one of the projects that reflect this beautiful picture that is AFiUK - the Ambassadors' Uhuru Project. Individuals and groups reaching out into the community, much further than two Kenyan girls could reach. Thank you to each and every ambassador that has contributed so far, and to all the other ambassadors that are going to enter and find a space to birth and nurture their visions. Karibuni!!

Jacqui Gitau
Co-Founding Director, African Families in the UK (AFiUK) CIC

Foreword

Did you know that all over the world there are ethnic minority communities that are still struggling to find the resources to grow their communities and help the people within them?

Rachel Walton, the author of *The Ambassador,* has made it her goal in life to help minority groups to better their own lives, and the lives of the people around them. She wants to provide communities with the resources to grow and, in turn, help other communities. If you want to make a big change, you need to make a big impact, and that is exactly what Rachel has done. She has paved the way to show that you can make anything happen if you put your mind to it, and have enough strength and courage to keep going.

In her book, Rachel shows you how she first started helping ethnic groups, and how quickly she saw a difference in these communities after realizing that she had to show the people in these communities how to pay it forward, and help others along the way.

Rachel created a program called "Community Ambassadors," through which she has helped countless individuals find a better path in life, and continue to educate themselves. She has first-hand knowledge of the good things that come from helping, and she wants to continue to make a difference in people's lives, each and every day.

Helping yourself and changing your life are wonderful goals, and when you are able to help yourself, you can also learn to help others. Then, wonderful things can start to happen, and you can truly start to see a shift of good. No matter who you are, or what you do, this book will give you the strength and passion to help others.

I encourage you to read *The Ambassador* today, and start learning about how amazing it is to help minority communities grow!

Raymond Aaron
New York Times Bestselling

Introduction

Neighbours and family are always amazed at how I skip, run, and navigate corners. Thus, my individual leadership purpose – skip-running for life, step-by-step – supports people to be connected with their divine destiny by creating the right opportunities for each individual. My passion stems from my faith: I believe I am a co-worker of the Creator.

I am a natural people developer and connector, and I am consistently inspired and excited when people's lives have been transformed while being connected with networks that make them flourish. This is my chosen 'authenticity adaptability' lifestyle conviction, carried with humility and compassion.

I took a course on Executive Leadership at Oxford University and one of the lecturers, Steve Mostyn, stated that you need to grow leaders, not just expect them to appear. This prompted me to remember that I needed to invest in growing myself. In 1993 I took a sabbatical for one year from my work with an Aviation Organisation (Mission Aviation Fellowship Kenya Programme) to be a missionary in Nigeria.

I was a young missionary in Nigeria and I remember my mentors Mr. Ofodile, the President of Child Evangelism Mission (CEM), and Jacqui Wesley (Everett) vividly telling me, "Multiply yourself, pass the 'mantle' to someone else, and always train a 'Timothy' and encourage 'Timothy' to pass that knowledge to someone else like a snowball." Recently, I even found myself listening to an audio by John Maxwell, and he echoes the same; growth of a leader is growing others.

This also reminded me of going to a conference called "Whom shall I send?" by FOCUS (Kenya), and an Advanced Leadership Course by Haggai

Institute in Hawaii. I answered both calls by saying, "Here I am, send me." That is how I started my journey.

I then became a Sunday School superintendent and had an impact on 54 Sunday School teachers. Then my Bishop, J.B. Masinde, and Mrs. Persiah Masinde, my mentor/coach, sent me to be a local missionary in the Redeemed Church denomination to equip Sunday School teachers.

Eventually, my childhood friend Jacqui Gitau and I registered African Families in the UK (AFiUK)CIC in 2015, built on the bedrock of improving the lives of Third Culture children and their families.

My personal purpose is also a reflection of my family. I have learned to allocate my energy, resources, and time firstly to my family. My husband Nigel and our son David are the backbone of my productivity, helping me fulfil my purpose. My skill set is fused with the joy that flows from my heart, which I use in service to others.

I have also learned to grow leaders who, in their own right, are empowering others, through a positive ripple effect. This saw the birth of Pastor Beth Waweru in Kenya leading a children's ministry of 1,200 children and 40 Sunday School teachers and 'Community Ambassador Model' in UK.

This book serves to explain my journey with AFiUK and the importance of our Community Ambassadors, who deliver a community-wide service to help to remove the barriers – and bridge the gap – for minorities who struggle to find a voice due to cultural, language and other differences.

Chapter 1

Closed Doors Conference

All over the world, there are Third Culture children, women and girls in minority communities who are in need of help and the knowledge to get themselves into a better situation. In 2015, my childhood friend Jacqui Gitau and I decided to start an organisation called African Families in the UK (AFiUK). Since registering AFiUK, we have been able to make an impact on many individuals and their families.

Our passion behind AFiUK is to create a new world for those that struggle to find their own voice. Not only do I want to help other families, I also want to give them the knowledge to pass onto others so that change can be made all over the world. I want to change people's lives and see where that takes them; to give them the power to make positive changes for themselves and future generations.

Initial Talks of Conference and Collaboration Between Stop the Traffik and African Families in the UK CIC (AFiUK)

In 2018, African Families in the UK(AFiUK)CIC co-founder Rachel Walton met with "Stop the Traffik – Modern Slavery and Human Trafficking" Community Coordinator, Kate Evans, to do collaborative work.

Stop the Traffik was interested in how to reach women and girls in minority communities who may be in difficult situations where they can be exploited, and may be isolated because of cultural and language barriers. They may be in the situation where they do not know their rights, or even how to get help.

AFiUK was also working to develop links within minority groups, and with helping organisations, so it seemed that there were similar interests and goals.

We knew that messages of help from organisations were not reaching vulnerable women and girls, and that there were barriers between communities and statutory organisations with a lack of trust and communication on both sides, so this is what we needed to repair.

Communities all around us had amazing, skilled, and inspirational people who had embedded themselves in their own communities and were trusted. We knew there were people in every community who could communicate with other community members, and organisations to begin building bridges.

We decided to find a way to make these issues known, and agreed that a conference would be a great way to raise awareness of women and girls in difficult situations. We decided to begin by looking at the issues of Child Sexual Exploitation, Domestic Servitude and Forced Marriage.

Closed Doors Conference

CONFERENCE BEHIND CLOSED DOORS - THE EXPLOITATION OF WOMEN AND GIRLS

Now that we have opened a can of worms, what do we do?

We sat down to plan the first conference, and looked at speakers who would set the pace for high performance and inspire the audience to be change agents. This took place on October 30th, 2019 and it was called Behind Closed Doors. We identified inspirational speakers for each topic – people who had experience in working with the issues – and we made sure all the speakers were from minority backgrounds.

We invited representatives from all the relevant BAME (Black, Asian and Minority Ethnic) groups, and professionals from appropriate statutory organisations and charities to start the process of raising awareness and building bridges.

2

At the conference, I delivered the following speech:

"The Cambridge dictionary explains 'opening a can of worms' as "a situation that causes a lot of problems for you when you start to deal with it: and can mean more trouble than you have bargained for."

AFiUK found domestic servitude, that is 'modern slavery,' as a serious and complicated problem. AFiUK was not willing to 'open up that can of worms' without the support and collaboration of funders, churches, police, agencies, statutory bodies, organisations and communities at large.

When you reflect on issues of domestic servitude – which are modern slavery, forced marriage, sexual exploitation – you almost enter an abyss of darkness, and this is a distressing place to be.

German philosopher Friedrich Nietzsche gave a warning, "Whoever fights monsters should see to it that in the process he does not become a monster. And if you gaze long enough into an abyss the abyss will gaze back at you."

There is a famous story about King George III, which provides an example of how small gestures and changes can make a big difference.

It tells how he would often spend time at Windsor Castle, walking about the grounds, sometimes paying surprise visits to his neighbours on the estate. On one of these visits, he came across a barn and found a woman milking a cow. She was unaware that she was being visited by the King. He asked her where all the other farm workers were. She replied that they had all gone to see the King, but she wasn't fussed about seeing him and she thought they were all fools for going because they would lose a day's work and she couldn't afford that as she had five children to provide for. King George took some coins from his pocket and gave them to her, saying that she could tell her friends, who had gone to see the King, that the King had been to see her.

Adapted from the original story - Christopher Hibbert, George III (London: Penguin, 1999),198

Now, to all who have come – decision makers, funders, churches, police, agencies, statutory bodies, organisations and community at large – can we say, with confidence, that by having your presence in this conference, that we have been visited by the King? Will you join together with us to fight domestic servitude, forced marriage, and sexual exploitation?

AFiUK is well placed in the community and is a key hub for working with ethnic minorities. AFiUK's collaboration with Stop the Traffik, the main lead organisation in this conference, provides an opportunity to strengthen our resolve to fight domestic servitude, forced marriage, and sexual exploitation of our women and girls.

We want to build partnerships and find solutions to better protect our women and girls. We need to step up our efforts to effect change. Change involves making agreements between diverse stakeholders of similar convictions in a course we all believe in.

The objective of this conference was to find:

- Diverse solutions
- Highly capable institutions to put robust policies and resources in place
- Funding streams
- Committed organisations/institutions which are already doing the work on ground, and strengthen our collaboration with them
* New innovative ways to combat sophisticated crime triangles in collaboration with the police
- More research to inform practical policies and interventions and to raise public awareness
- Ways to provide education to key stakeholders and to empower and positively challenge them on the issues at hand
- Ways to work with the media to profile stories to support advocacy and campaigning

And finally, we are looking to find ways to "plant the trees from which we may not enjoy the shade, but that other generations will benefit from."- *Hyacinthe Loyson (1866)*

Therefore, we are calling on all our intelligence, organisations, statutory bodies, police, funders, churches, and community at large to have collective responsibility to win this war. It is time to treat the illegal organised trade as it is, by understanding the motion passed on modern slavery in September 2018.

"Modern slavery damages economic growth and sustainable economic development. It undermines governance and the rule of law. It robs communities & businesses of their future way of well-being and income."
First Lady Margaret Kenyatta

AFiUK intends to help reduce domestic servitude, forced marriage, and sexual exploitation by stepping up their efforts and tackling organised crime. This can happen by supporting Stop the Traffik, the main lead organisation, and further collaborating with local communities to increase their investment towards the protection of our women and girls.

In conclusion, we are adding AFiUK's voice to support our joint pledge towards this global fight and reaffirming AFIUK's commitment at all levels. I am inviting you to ACTION by cracking the party poppers, so that together we are saying, "We will do it" and we will celebrate our efforts soon by saying that freedom is coming tomorrow for our girls and our women.

Speakers for the Conference:

- Working to prevent the exploitation of girls and women – Mr. Nazir Afzal OBE – Former Chief Executive Police & Crime Commissioner.
- Working with forced marriage and domestic servitude – Ms. Bal Kaur Howard – Former PPO for Honour Based Violence Suffolk Police
- Tackling domestic servitude in Lewisham – Ms. Rachel Onikosi – Former Lewisham Councillor
- Supporting vulnerable victims – the role of the Solicitor – Ms. Ashlee Campbell of Fisher, Jones Greenwood Solicitors
- Future Planning – Rachel Walton AFiUK & Kate Evans STT

After the conference it was clear that participants had been engaged and were asking, "What can we do?" We looked at what the next step should be, and knew it was important that whatever we did would be based on what was identified by community members who understood cultural issues and knew best how to reach their communities. In AFiUK, we were already experienced in bringing diverse communities together, and were aware of how to engage people.

Leadership styles are very important in order to know how to engage a community, and this enables you to be able to reach out to said community. We went back to the previous communities we had visited, and since in our organisation we practice a leadership style which is participatory, this means from the inception of a project, our community is engaged in consultation and creation of the service.

For example, in a pandemic crisis such as COVID-19, we have engaged our followers in a delegative approach since we realized to some degree that culture informs pandemic responses. The followers have both local and cultural knowledge to communicate successful response measures in the format their communities understand.

My preferred leadership style is participatory. I find myself modelling through engaging in committees, associations, events and forums run by my followers, where passion, problem solving, responsibility and decision making is shared. I like this approach because my followers start having a sense of ownership and belonging and, as a result, they radiate positive energy that is felt in the whole organisation.

Servant and transformational approaches are our models since our organisation exists to bridge the gap and meet the needs of our followers and transform their lives. We seek to support our followers by ensuring they value their own skills, knowledge and experience.

We have actively listened to the community and are discerning the situation on ground. We know that domestic servitude, sexual exploitation, and forced marriage are very sensitive topics, so knowing when to adapt to different leadership styles is very important.

Reflective Questions

What leadership style do you use and why?

Would you use different approaches with women and men, and why?

Chapter Two

Open Doors Conference

What Next? What Can We Do?

We had been asked the questions, "What can we do?" and "What next?"

We knew that our next steps should be guided by participants, so we decided we would have a second conference, but this would be a BAME community conference, with speakers and workshops, discussing issues and making recommendations about "What next?" that would be relevant to those specific communities.

Open Doors Conference

We held the Opening Doors Conference on March 12th, 2019, and this was to address both safeguarding issues and the support of vulnerable women and girls.

We wanted to educate women of all ages and give them the opportunity to better their own lives, and the lives of women around them. Our goal was to guide them on the right path, so that positive changes could be made.

This conference was funded by the National Lottery Awards for All Fund. Four empowering speakers from a range of backgrounds spoke about the work of social care with BAME families, FGM, modern slavery and the building of an empowerment project from lived experience. Two of the speakers demonstrated as leaders and trainers that they were strong, successful and powerful women, who were using their lived experience to empower others.

Throughout this conference, we wanted to stay focused on several important topics. These included a discussion on safeguarding vulnerable young people, which was run by Ms. Adwoa Solomon. She wanted to make females aware of domestic abuse, and how to keep themselves and their families safe if they ever found themselves in a dangerous situation.

Our second topic had to do with forced marriage and domestic servitude, and this discussion was led by Ms. Bal Kaur Howard, who was the former PPO for Honour Based Violence Suffolk Police. Her goal was to share her own story and experiences, as well as explain to women that there are choices, and they have the choice to lead the life they want.

The third topic we felt was important was about managing and responding to risk, which was discussed by Ms. Rohma Ullah, the National Lead for Training and Professional Development. Her goal was to give advice that would assist front line practitioners. She wanted to give tools to these women that would help them in both their personal and professional lives.

The final topic was about discovering the kind of support communities around us needed, to help close the gaps and start opening up the barriers that people in these communities have had. Dr. Muzvare Hazvipen Betty Makoni, the Director of Girls Empowerment Initiative, ran this discussion, and wanted to find out what it would take to start making big changes in these communities, and what steps really needed to be taken to make a difference in people's lives.

Additionally, the speakers also wanted to take some time to have a discussion on what in general makes women and girls in BAME communities vulnerable, and what the gaps or barriers are, that are blocking them from providing proper support and safeguarding. These are the important questions that we strived to find answers for.

Participants became passionately involved, and there was a lot of feedback and advice after the conference; many issues that make women and girls vulnerable were identified. The lack of trust in, and communication with, providers of statutory services was highlighted, and the importance of the cultural context identified.

From this we developed recommendations to answer the question of "What to do next?" We did know what we wanted to improve, but did not know exactly how to get there. We believed that links should be built between Statutory Services and BAME groups so that we could improve trust, increase understanding, and support cultural awareness.

We also knew how important it was to educate young girls and women. We wanted to be able to give females proper education and public awareness in schools, different communities and via professionals. This was an important step to make sure that women of all ages were aware of the services provided, and how to get help if needed.

When looking at our communities, we noticed a lot of guidance was needed to give people a way to improve their lives, and the lives of those around them. Many communities do not have the information on what to do, where to go, and what supports are available. So, we knew that this type of guidance would be an important addition to give others in these communities.

As a team, we wanted to provide many more opportunities to women and girls so that they could gain the knowledge to show themselves the steps to having a healthy, safe, and happy life. We had seen first-hand that if groups of people come together to communicate a similar interest or goal, then they can eventually build links, or friendships, and develop more advocates for girls and women.

It had also come to our attention that we were focusing mainly on women and girls. After coming to this conclusion, we decided it would be important for men and boys to also be a part of this conversation about change and growth. We knew we had to come up with some sort of arrangement that included both men and women, ensuring that the environment was made conducive for everyone, so that everyone would feel that they could open up and be part of the conversation.

We eventually agreed on what our next steps from the conference should be, and we initially thought that forming an advisory group would be a great decision so that we could start to develop an empowerment project. This project would be aimed at linking statutory service providers with BAME groups to identify certain ways of improving practice in safeguarding vulnerable women and girls in the BAME communities.

We knew the great importance of creating conversations around BAME communities, and how to start making positive changes. We also wanted to start looking into developing a BAME hub in Colchester, UK, so that we could ensure we were making as much of an impact as possible.

The empowerment project included a plan to offer some community activist training, and community awareness training so that we could increase understanding of safeguarding law, and avenues of help.

Throughout this time, we had been working with men to help us with developing a Men and Boys conference. Since many of our women and men may have had past problems with the opposite sex, we knew having a separate conference would probably be the best option, to avoid any mixed emotions coming up. We wanted a safe haven for all to open up and express what was on their minds, in an environment that felt safe and comfortable.

Lastly, we wanted to create more avenues and opportunities to have meetings for continued conversation. We wanted to increase these meetings so that they were available on both weekends and evenings. This would give the community members an opportunity to involve themselves in these meetings and become more aware of the issues in their own community.

My Speech at Conclusion of Conference:

In today's Opening Doors Conference 2019, we were building blocks on the foundation of the Closed-Door Conference 2018 and putting structure in place.

From the feedback we have collected from the workshops today, Kate Evans of Stop the Traffik and I will take action and report to Safer Colchester Partnership, the Police, Community360 and the Safeguarding Board.

We will continue actively listening to you because together we will have a collective voice, be heard, be powerful, be the difference, be a vessel that can be used to make change.

In conclusion, "Mothers and daughters together are a powerful force to be reckoned with." Melia Keeton-Digby, The Heroines Club: A Mother-Daughter Empowerment Circle

Envision and Engaging

We needed to capture and build on the enthusiasm and passion from the two conferences, and to distil the clear messages that we had heard, to take back to the community to start envisioning, engaging, sharing and communicating the vision.

We wanted to be able to enrich BAME families by equipping, developing, transforming, and adding value to each of their lives. We saw the importance in equipping their lives by providing resources and tools that increased their capability to shape their communities.

We knew that the way to transform lives in such a diverse community was by fully engaging the Community Ambassadors, who we had already identified and spotted their potential and talent, and therefore had to develop them in a person-centred way that was relevant to their individual needs.

It was important to develop their lives through transferring knowledge and offering training to Community Ambassadors, who in their own right would empower others in a positive ripple effect, reaching out to all branches of hitherto unchartered territories in the community.

Our goal was to show others our vision and let them see the importance of this for themselves, so they felt engaged enough to let others in the community know. We were adding value to their lives by inspiring, creating a conducive environment, providing the right opportunities, nurturing and coaching the leader that resides within each Community Ambassador, all to empower them and connect them to networks and teams to flourish in their area of calling.

To get people in the communities more engaged and ready to make a difference, we had to find a way to properly communicate what we were trying to get across.

13

To begin with, I felt it was important to let others know who I am in this vision. I believe in our vision to the fullest, and look at myself as authentic. I am a walking visual vision carrier, consistent, and an open book that followers can communicate with and read easily.

Our leaders and followers also needed to know where and how this information was given. Mainly, I shared our vision through team meetings, one-to-one conversations and coaching. We also shared our vision through inspirational testimonials, community groups, and events.

The way we chose to share our information was also important. We decided it was the best option to create a leaflet and video clip so that people interested in our Uhuru Project could have information about us that was easily accessible.

With regard to language, we knew that there might be some confusion if someone else did not know a certain language. As a result, we chose to use the application called WhatsApp, so that no matter what, everyone could be understood, and their words could be expressed properly.

There were so many ways in which we wanted to get our vision across, but knew we would have to find a general way to do so because of the fact that, all over the world, there are not only a vast number of languages spoken, but there are also different cultures, and different opinions. It is because of the passion to make a difference that this organisation has become what it is today.

Reflective Questions

What different ways are there to ensure that people want to become involved and engaged with a project?

How would you ensure that everyone gets their voice heard in a workshop setting?

How can a vision be communicated in a persuasive way to embrace the diverse cultures?

Chapter Three

Engagement

Engagement Between Main-Line Service Providers and Community Leaders

Community leaders and ambassadors understand that communication is key; therefore, they ensure that their communities have relevant information presented in a suitable format, and support to overcome barriers in accessing local services.

Mainline service providers need to understand that relationships with ethnic minority organisations are key. They need to value ethnic minority individuals for who they are, respecting their local knowledge and skills.

Therefore, it calls upon mainline service providers to seek ways to understand and engage with diverse communities through their community leaders. One of the ways to do this is by working in collaboration with ethnic minority organisations and have them communicate and conduct themselves in ways that build trust.

Secondly, if they are to challenge behaviours and beliefs that are accepted as 'norms and mores' within a culture, one has to be respectful and sensitive, and seek the guidance of community leaders and ambassadors. This would help mainline service providers gain access to a community where they can then come in and give the help that is necessary.

This was re-emphasised in a conference by the police called *Together Working, Together Standing* in 2016. One of the speakers, who was an intervention provider, emphasized the importance of young people being engaged in sports or employment to prevent them from getting groomed or radicalized.

Tess Wisbey, the Essex Prevent Engagement Officer, had this to say: "It is important that, when young vulnerable people are identified within Essex, we are able to link them to social activities that not only offer them friendship but also the skills needed to move on with life, study and career paths. If these opportunities are also delivered by community leaders that have a good grounding in cultural and religious needs, it can only support our communities' development."

We have inequalities in health, race, gender, economy and education, among other issues. We need main service providers co-creating services with community leaders and community ambassadors.

AFiUK is offering Cultural Awareness workshops to professionals and practitioners. Those who attend would benefit in a multitude of ways, including:

- increasing knowledge and understanding of working with diverse communities
- developing understanding of inter-cultural competence on issues affecting diverse communities
- encouraging communication between professionals and BAME during the co-creating process
- developing skills to work with interpreters during the co-creating process
- increasing confidence in working with diverse communities
- increasing understanding on how to take account of culture, ethnicity and race when it comes to safeguarding processes
- addressing under- or over-representation of the take-up of services
- improving access to local services

The Community Ambassador programme highlights various inequalities that affect communities; it is a prime example of how raising awareness can help bridge the gaps between diverse ethnic groups and public services, and strengthen links between communities.

"The design and implementation of policy, on both a local or national level, should always be well informed and carried out with a developed understanding of the complexity of the diverse communities."
– Cllr. Susan Barker Culture, Communities and Customer Member CC

Engagement Between Community Leaders and the Ambassadors

Our organisation prides itself on the leaders and ambassadors in the communities that we work with. They create positive energy and enthusiasm and from the very start, we knew that the women in these communities would play a major role in the changes we wanted to make. It was just a matter of finding people who were a right fit and who would help empower other people in their communities to start making a difference.

We recruited Community Ambassadors by asking women who were already active in their communities, and respected as community leaders, to identify people they thought might be interested in spreading the word through churches, the Mosque, community gatherings etc. We produced a leaflet with contact details, so that information could be given out to people throughout these communities.

Eleven women were eventually identified from a range of backgrounds, who would be perfect for involvement in our organisation. They completed a volunteer form which identified why they were interested in the project, and what previous experience they had, and we all met together to talk about the background of the project, and key discussion points from the previous conference.

We were clear that we wanted this to be led by the women themselves. The community leaders also went on to our Advisory Group, ensuring that the women who came forward would have a voice in the process, without deferring to the stronger voices of respected elders.

This led to our group of women deciding they wanted to be known as Community Ambassadors, and choosing how they wanted to be represented. They chose a logo, which was a sunflower, a flower that stands tall and turns its face to the sun. We also discussed what languages would be included with the symbol, as we thought it was important to show different cultures and languages, all brought together.

The group also co-designed a leaflet and a banner which would be used at events. They had to think carefully about the wording on the leaflet, which would identify that they wanted to support women, but recognised that for many women, the permission from husbands and senior family members had to be sought before they could take part. This enabled our women to gel as a group, with an agreed common purpose.

In addition, we met with each person individually to look at their individual knowledge, skills, experience and needs, using an outcome pathway to identify how confident they felt. We identified a range of training that would give Community Ambassadors a good grounding in working with vulnerable women, and a range of information they would need. We recognized that some already had a good basis of training and would not need to attend every training session; it all depended on the individual.

We also provided opportunities to attend conferences and other groups. For example, the Community Ambassadors were all invited to a Rah Theatre performance and discussion about modern slavery, which communicated the message through drama; and two lead Community Ambassadors were invited to be part of the Independent Advisory Group (IAG), which links police and other statutory bodies to communities.

Ambassadors were invited to attend all community celebration events with a stall where they could meet people and explain their work. At a Rice and Spice Festival, Ambassadors invited women to write *Women are amazing because...* and *One brave thing I am going to do over the next year...* and pin these on a board. This led to many conversations, and allowed many women who participated to actually speak their mind and feel like they were being heard.

"Good things happen to a team when a player takes the place
where he adds the most value. Great things happen when
all the players on the team take the role that maximizes their strengths
—their talent, skill, and experience."
– Dr. John C. Maxwell

Culture and Community Ambassadors

AFiUK and Stop the Traffik came together to build a collaborative and adaptive culture. The two organisations worked together in partnership, bringing two diverse organisations together to work on a common goal.

The Community Ambassadors make a huge impact on our communities. For example, during the Covid-19 pandemic, our Community Ambassador teams took care of each other by creating AFiUK's Adopt a Neighbour scheme. This was very successful and involved adopting a key worker's child to enable the parent to serve the nation, or a foreign student who could not go back to their origin home due to border closures.

Charitable work is a choice and a lifestyle. It is a service, and its followers are passionate and share a common cause. They are one another's keeper; they know the extended families of the clients they work with, since social capital is essential in BAME families.

We have adapted the idea of the growth mindset concept, which is a person's belief in their own ability to learn and grow their skills without the need of focusing on natural ability. Instead, they focus on determination and hard work. Our organisation thrives on both professional competencies and local cultural knowledge/competencies possessed by Community Ambassadors, and growing our communities' mindset, which is important for pursuing our current and future opportunities.

We embarked on building on these strengths, investing in a coach who develops every individual in a person-centred way, and enrolling followers/leaders in relevant courses. Through this collaboration, we have offered excellent services, outdoing ourselves as well as being able to respond to the constant changing environment we live and work in. We are able to meet the community gaps identified, achieving alignment and reinforcing the core organisational constituents we have created.

"I have been honoured to be a Master of Ceremony of
one of the Women's Conferences that was organised by AFiUK,
and a speaker to the Community Ambassadors. I encouraged them
to stand and be counted and to be women of courage."
– Rev. Beckie Baraka

Furthermore, we have developed a dynamic and active Community Ambassador team who, in their own right, are now empowering others through a positive ripple effect, reaching out to all branches of hitherto unchartered territories in their communities.

AFiUK, working in collaboration with Stop the Traffik, opened doors for other opportunities for funding streams and connected with the organisations they were working with, which we wouldn't have been able to know about without their help. This collaboration was beneficial to our Community Ambassadors and the wider community.

The interaction and shared vision and learning from Stop the Traffik was very enriching for AFiUK. This collaboration added value to AFiUK, and together we came up with the Uhuru Project, the renowned Community Ambassador model.

Reflective Questions

How can you transform your engagement with the community?

What are the local/cultural knowledge gaps?

How can you involve individuals and communities with lived experiences in the development and delivery of your projects?

Chapter 4

Uhuru Project – Community Ambassadors

"All our dreams can come true, if we have the courage to pursue them."
– Walt Disney

Recruitment Process and the Birth of the Uhuru Project

If you look at most organisations, when you recruit a volunteer, you recruit one individual, one person. When it comes to community-based organisations, however, when you recruit a person, you are not only recruiting that person individually, but you are also indirectly recruiting the entire community that surrounds them.

When looking within minority ethnic communities, you have to seek the counsel of the gatekeepers; the members of the community that are trusted and whom others look to for support. It is important to ensure that a community volunteer is accepted and supported within their community. Community work is all about social capital, and the depth of your relationships with the gatekeepers of said community.

Uhuru, which means freedom in Swahili, was exactly what our project wanted to focus on. Freedom was our main focus, due to the fact that we wanted both women and men of all ages to live to their fullest potential and know that they are free to be whoever they want to be.

The vision for the project was about mainly two things. Firstly, we wanted to make sure that women and girls of all ages were able to access support if at any time they required it. We wanted to be there first-hand to help within their communities in culturally sensitive ways.

The second major part of our vision was that we wanted to establish trust within other multi-agencies who helped others in a similar manner. Our goal was to build bridges with other agencies to ensure we could all work in a culturally appropriate way.

Within our organisation, two separate groups needed to be built. These were the Advisory Group of professionals, and the community volunteers. Having these groups working together would help make this project truly successful, and help ensure that a difference could be made.

As I have already outlined in Chapter Three, through consultation, it was decided that community volunteers would be called Community Ambassadors, as they were to be the bridge to build trust. The Cambridge dictionary meaning of ambassador is *an accredited diplomat sent by a state as its permanent representative in a foreign country*, which we found to be very fitting, considering what our Ambassadors would be doing.

We made a leaflet asking women if they were interested in becoming a Community Ambassador and we ensured that the leaflets had pictures of women of all ages from diverse communities, so that no matter what the age, all women would come and feel like they were recognized and welcomed.

When it came to the women who would be selected as our Community Ambassadors, we wanted to make sure that they would stand out for a reason. Firstly, we wanted to have these women come from different communities and faiths across Colchester. We knew this was our best chance of making a real difference within these communities.

We wanted our Ambassadors to take part in events and celebrations throughout different communities, to show the strength of women in those communities. As an organisation, we felt it was important to demonstrate the strength of women to give others the confidence to start opening up and sharing their stories with others too. This would hopefully create a chain of events where women were helping each other and giving one another strength.

It was also important that our Community Ambassadors were a positive voice for women and girls in communities, to help ensure that all their needs were understood. There are so many women around the world who do not have the confidence to use their voice to make a difference. We felt our Community Ambassadors needed to be that voice to show women that a change could be made – as long as you used your voice in a productive and uplifting way.

The women who were to be the Community Ambassadors were going to be a signpost for women and girls who might need some extra support to navigate the systems set in place. The Community Ambassadors were going to be the first point of contact for their communities to help women of all ages. If the Ambassadors could make a difference in women's lives, the chain would continue, and women in different communities would then learn to help others. This was our goal for this Uhuru Project.

We decided on a total of eleven Ambassadors, and these women were recruited from diverse community groups, and a diverse range of ages and backgrounds. Within those eleven Ambassadors, three of which were the Community Lead Ambassadors who would sit on the Advisory Board once formed.

Some of these Ambassadors came with both qualifications and experience, which we knew would be a great asset to us as they already had something of an idea of what we wanted to accomplish.

Although not all the Ambassadors had the recommended qualifications, they all came with cultural unique competencies that could not be replaced by professional intervention. They all knew the goal, and they had the passion to make it happen. It was amazing knowing we had started out this journey to make a huge impact on these small ethnic minority communities.

"Collaboration is important not just because it's a better way to learn.
The spirit of collaboration is penetrating every institution and all of our lives.
So, learning to collaborate is part of equipping yourself for effectiveness,
problem solving, innovation and life-long learning
in an ever-changing networked economy."
– Don Tapscott

Our next step was making sure that the Advisory Group was completed and fully set up with the Uhuru Project ready to take off. To make this happen, we needed to obtain a grant. We applied to the National Lottery Fund *Awards for All Grants*.

After successfully obtaining our National Lottery Fund *Awards for All Grants*, we had to get our Uhuru Project started by setting the Advisory Group in place. We started off with the Colchester Borough Council.

We felt it was important for them to be included because we wanted to align our organisation with the Council's Community Enabling Strategy Officer, and together we would achieve our common goals of improving the lives of our communities within the Borough. We needed them to support the Uhuru project initiative and see our vision – and see the importance of it – so that they would be able to assist us at any point throughout this process, if need be.

Other important aspects of our Advisory Group were groups that assisted with the wellbeing of children and youth. We considered the Children's Social Care and the Youth Offending Service to assist us with our Uhuru Project. Since children were a major reason why we created this project, we felt the need to have other professionals on our side was essential, so that along the way, we could create more of an impact.

Since girls and women were such an important aspect of the Uhuru Project, we thought that CARA would be another important charity to add to our Advisory Group, to offer specialist support for victims and survivors of child abuse and sexual violence.

Another organisation which we had interest working with was a group called Refugee Action. Their main purpose for running their organisation is to help and support refugees and assist with leading a more productive life in the UK. We believed they were important because there are so many people, not just women, who are in need of finding a better life for their families after leaving their past life behind.

A major part of our own organisation's mission is protecting both adults and children from harm and abuse. This is what the NHS England Safeguarding

Team focuses on, so we felt it was important for us to work alongside with them as well.

Lastly, because of the fact that we work so closely with ethnic minority communities, we wanted to ensure we had a representation from the police force, with an officer from the Hate Crime Department. This officer would assist in training the Community Ambassadors on how to raise awareness of hate crime in their communities, and how victims of hate crime can report it.

Knowing how vital the police partnership would be in our work, I set out to be introduced to the Chief Inspector of police. Below is the email exchange that we had:

To: *Elliott Judge D/SUPT*
Subject: *Request for Introduction*
Dear Insp. Elliot,
"I hope this finds you well. I would like to request if you would introduce me to the current Colchester Chief Inspector of Police Rob Huddleston. There is a local police meeting which will be happening in Colchester on 21st June and I will be going for it because the local police priorities match with our work in Colchester as you have witnessed before."
Regards
Rachel Walton
BAME Community Development Consultant/Co-Founder
African Families in the UK (AFiUK) CIC

Hi Rob,
Please see the email above from Rachel Walton (BAME Community Development Consultant/Co-Found African Families in the UK (AFiUK) CIC).
Rachel is an absolute asset to Colchester and is somebody that helped me to reach out to so many during my time in Colchester.
She is really keen to make contact with you and has requested that if possible you give her a call.
Regards
Elliott Judge
Detective Superintendent
Head of Operations and Proactive, Crime & Public Protection Command
Essex Police Headquarters PO Box 2, Springfield, Chelmsford, Essex, CM2 6DA

We knew that our organisation would not run smoothly if we did not have resources, contacts, and the knowledge available to help us along the way. We knew it would take a strong force to make a difference, and with the connections we had made, we were on the right path.

The aim of the Advisory Group was to oversee the Uhuru Project, and to link the project to Statutory and Voluntary Organisations for sustainability. We wanted that connection so that we could give advice, support, and offer training as needed, or appropriate.

Reflective Questions

What are the benefits of an Advisory Group?

What organisations or individuals can you collaborate with to form an Advisory Group?

What is the importance of voluntary sector collaborating or partnering with the local police or local authorities?

How can the voluntary sector go about requesting a statutory sector partner to be committed in supporting sustainability of their projects?

Chapter 5

Investment

"Start from wherever you are and with whatever you've got."
− Jim Rohn

Uhuru Project Begins

The Uhuru Project was born and Community Ambassadors and the Advisory Group were recruited, with funding obtained from National Lottery *Awards for All* Fund. We embarked on building on the strengths of the dynamic and active Community Ambassadors, the investment from National Lottery *Awards for All* Fund and the Advisory Group. We knew that together we would be able to respond to the constant changing environment to meet the service gaps we would identify along the way.

The journey towards being effective in the local communities where we were working started here. We needed to set goals, underlying principles, aims, training and objectives. Effectiveness is viewed in our organisation when the pathways we have put in place are applied and manifested. That is with a multiplication of Community Ambassadors, social capital and an inclusive society and a proactive citizenship culture.

For example, the Uhuru Project initiative (Community Ambassador Model vision) was the development of a dynamic and active, diverse Community Ambassadors team. The programme builds on existing strengths, that is, their unique cultural competencies that cannot be replaced by competent professional intervention, and also focuses on capacity and capability. This team would reach out to all branches of hitherto unchartered territories in the Black Asian Minority and Refugee (BAMER) communities.

We started building on a framework that would provide a foundation on which the Uhuru Project – Advisory Group and Community Ambassadors – could co-create programmes with other communities. The structure of the Uhuru Project would reflect the relationships with other multi-agencies and institutions.

> *"Let our advance worrying become advance thinking and planning."*
> – Winston Churchill

> *"Hold the vision, trust the process."*
> – Anonymous

Ambassador Vision

To ensure that women, young women and girls in minority communities who are vulnerable and isolated through barriers of language, gender inequality, knowledge of rights and resources, power imbalance and lack of trust, will have access to information and support that is appropriate for their needs.

Minority community representatives will support professionals to enhance awareness of cultural and faith contexts, and trust and communication will improve.

To communicate the vision in a compelling way to the community meant that as leaders we had to believe and know it as the back of our hand; be inspirational and passionate, radiate positive energy, and engage with all our followers. The vision would be part and parcel of the follower's own engagement and understanding of what we were about.

Underlying Principles

When it comes to our beliefs, we are truly aware that it is the people, their families, and their communities that have unique competencies that never could be replaced by any sort of professional intervention. It is the people that live in those communities that know best how to improve them; they just need the resources to do so.

While professionals may eventually come to a solution, they have a tendency to focus on the negative, or what is wrong with a situation. Our project intends to do the opposite. We want to start focusing on what is strong in communities. We want to support and empower women to make them stronger, and confident to keep spreading the word and make positive changes in other people's lives.

For the communities to feel they belong, and have a sense of ownership of the Uhuru project, the Advisory Group & Community Ambassadors will embark on co-creating services with the communities they belong to.

To create a more inclusive society, the Advisory Group should actively listen, understand and value the skills, local/cultural knowledge and experience of the Community Ambassadors.

The Uhuru Project's guiding principles include servant leadership, integrity, planning, respect of diversity, lifelong learning, collaboration, shared learning, shared vision, shared mission and our passion to make a difference within the communities we work with and belong to.

Aims of Project

"If you aim at nothing, you will hit it every time."
— Zig Ziglar

Our project had so many goals we wanted to accomplish, but we knew not everything could be done immediately; many of the changes have been gradual but were incredibly impactful right from the start.

From the very beginning of this project, we knew first and foremost our goal was to empower, equip, and build on existing strengths within minority communities so that we could support vulnerable women and girls of all ages. We wanted to accomplish this through the opportunities provided through our Community Ambassadors, positioned to be able to provide advocacy and support communities to access specialist culturally appropriate services and networks.

The Uhuru Project also intended on linking Statutory and Voluntary Organisation partners to our Community Ambassadors so that we could ensure that diverse solutions were set in place. This also included linking with multi-agency initiatives to make sure that robust and appropriate policies, procedures and pathways were properly prepared and that there would be no issues along the way.

"Knowledge is exploding,
so you need to commit yourself to a plan for lifelong learning."
– Don Tapscott

Training and Agency Links

Within our organisation, we wanted to ensure that we had enough training set in place so there were no snags along the way. Due to the fact that so many of the women and children that would be involved in our organisation had been through some kind of trauma, we wanted our Community Ambassadors to be aware of anything and everything that could possibly emerge, while working with the people in these communities.

To start with, we felt there was a major need for confidence building, not only with the people we meet in these minority communities, but also the women and girls who became Community Ambassadors, or at least more involved within our organisation. We wanted to build their confidence so that they felt like they were able to make a change and know that they could be successful with it.

In order to ensure that training was relevant to Community Ambassadors and would give them a good framework, we met with each individual to look at their existing knowledge, skills, experience and interests, and level of confidence. This was an interesting experience, as within some communities, women can be very self-effacing and modest, but also possess a real depth of knowledge and understanding.

Through active listening exercises, we were able to identify gaps and mind map the training they needed as a group. Additionally, it was evident that to develop every Community Ambassador in a person-centred way, we needed to have a one to one coaching and mentoring scheme in place as well.

Community Ambassadors also needed to have awareness of victim support, and mental health first aid due to the increased need of care in this sector. There was a lengthy list of topics that could be brought up throughout discussions in communities, so we needed to make sure that our Ambassadors would feel confident, and have the knowledge to help people in need, whatever the subject.

There also needed to be a focus on abuse and the many ways abuse shows its face, such as hate crimes, domestic abuse, sexual abuse, and even modern slavery. Many of these topics are extremely sensitive, so ensuring those discussing these topics were well prepared was an important part of the training process.

We wanted to strive to develop these communities in a positive way, so that every single person had the knowledge to not only better their own lives, but also pass on the knowledge, and help others in the future.

"Good business leaders create a vision, articulate the vision, passionately own the vision, and relentlessly drive it to completion."
– Jack Welch

The Plan

When the Advisory Group was set up, eleven women from different communities came forward to be Community Champions. They undertook training from agencies about what help they could offer to increase their knowledge, and this included safeguarding training. This also enabled them, with those agencies, to look at how their services could better meet the needs of women in their communities.

The major need identified for these women in this role was to build their confidence and self-esteem. Doing this would ultimately help women create better lives for themselves and accomplish goals they would normally veer away from. Giving women and children the confidence to be who they want to be in life was our main priority.

In Phase Two, they planned to organise an event, *Women's Voices, aimed at* the BAME community, and use this to build up confidence through the skills needed to achieve this. We wanted to make it possible for them to develop confidence in public speaking; organisation skills, including developing publicity within their communities; liaising with other organisations; contacting stallholders, speakers, and caterers; thinking about the outcomes they wanted to achieve; and to deliver a successful project, which engaged with other women in their communities.

The *Women's Voices* event was postponed due to the global pandemic but the Community Ambassadors continued refining their services and taking them to homes through Zoom, WhatsApp, Google Meet, and Microsoft Teams platforms.

We achieved this by enlisting and paying for the support of experts to guide them through the process, and ongoing group work through a skilled practitioner aimed at building self-confidence.

Impact

Phase Two of the project would build on the initial work to develop the Uhuru Project, to raise the skills and confidence of women in minority communities who have come forward as Community Ambassadors to help them to undertake this role.

The expected outcome of this was that they would feel able to fulfil this role with confidence. In fact, this did not only support them as individuals, but in turn impacted on other women in their communities, often who had difficulties and were in circumstances where they did not know how to seek help.

Giving women and children the resources to better themselves and their lives can have a great impact on communities around us because these skills and confidence training can be passed on through word of mouth.

Many of these small communities are connected and people know everyone in their communities. Passing on these skills to other generations is what we strived for, but we knew this would obviously take some time if we were going to make the huge impact we had in mind.

There was already interest from other women who wanted to get involved, so, as this project was already succeeding, we were recruiting more Community Ambassadors, using the learning from this pilot. Later on, we were able to reciprocate this model in other organisations and towns.

We believe, therefore, that this can impact on many other vulnerable women in the future, both in terms of their confidence, but also in terms of their well-being and mental health support.

We planned to open confidence building sessions to other women, as identified and appropriate during the course of this project, and support women who want to take some of our sessions into their communities, ensuring that the impact of everything we have learned is shared effectively to relevant audiences.

Evidence

The key objective was to see an increase in confidence and self-esteem in our Ambassadors, and for that to be observable in their ability to develop skills and to deliver successful events. This would produce a feeling of success, which would be measured by the feedback from the events they run.

The Ambassadors have already met us on a one-on-one basis, and we looked with them at their confidence levels. This was in the form of a pathway plan where they were invited to score themselves on where they were on a range of issues, such as confidence in talking to professionals, and their own knowledge of different statutory services.

We will repeat this, looking at specific areas of confidence and well-being, so that we have a pathway plan for each woman, in order for them to be able to track their score of increases in confidence over time.

We will also report on the training and support they have undertaken, and ask them to evaluate this; which skills they have been offered; what the strengths, barriers and difficulties have been; and what we can all learn from this.

We will measure how many beneficiaries there are, how many other women have come forward to join a new group, how many women in communities reached with information, how many women attend the final conference, and what the feedback is from attendees and from the women themselves.

Added Value

The project exists to support vulnerable women in communities who may not have a voice, and may need help and support. There are many barriers identified in the workshops at the Opening Doors conference, including language, culture, isolation and lack of knowledge of their rights and the help available.

Building the skills and self-esteem of women within communities who can reach out to others to offer information and support has additional value. This is not only for women that they speak to but it also ensures that information is available in appropriate languages and formats in places that they go, including businesses, faith groups, and shops.

They will also be a bridge for helping statutory and other agencies who find BAME communities hard to reach, about how they can get specific messages across, or help to tailor their services differently. This adds value to those agencies and the work they do.

This pilot project for one small group of women carries the intention that another group will be recruited in the future. As women see that this is a helpful project, we expect that others will join. The reach will get bigger over time.

The conference is the culmination of the work to build skills and confidence and where we also hope that women will be awarded their Ambassador certificates. It will also add value, as this will bring issues to a wider audience of women recruited from these communities, and showcase role models of women who are now at the front and centre of the organisation.

Sustainability

The investment in this group of Ambassadors, in terms of the skills and knowledge they now possess, will be long-lasting within their community. People within these communities can continue to pass on their knowledge to newer generations, which will have a permanent impact on everyone. Volunteers rooted throughout these communities enables us to make the biggest impact possible.

We will continue to link them to local organisations who have seen the mutual benefit of our work and will provide training and support. These links should be sustainable into the future. When these links and pathways are clearly established into communities, this should be helpful for all.

For the first phase of recruitment, we were fortunate to obtain a National Lottery *Awards for All* grant. For the next phase of confidence and skills building we hope to be supported through this fund again and we hope to evaluate the learning from this pilot, with the intention of recruiting at least one more group next year.

During that time, we plan to work on other sources of income for the future with other groups, including exploring funds for a hub for our communities which our Ambassadors would link to.

This project is intended to be sustainable through making links between communities and other organisations. For example, our Community Ambassadors are working alongside NHS Midwives on their Midwives Model of Care to ensure that all pregnant women and girls access this vital support.

Phase 2 of the Uhuru Project was developed, and Essex Community Foundation supported it through their Tampon Tax Fund. Our next steps included drafting a plan, our goals, and the impact we wanted to make in the communities and people around us.

Project Uhuru implementation Phase 2: We had prepared the infrastructure by ensuring we had recruited both Community Ambassadors and Advisory Group. Now it was time to continue implementing more robust training for the Community Ambassadors, new processes and procedures, and coordinate with the organisations that we would collaborate with.

One of the core values we established was lifelong learning, and we continued training the Community Ambassadors on this Phase 2 of the project. This began with proper goal setting, so we knew the direction in which we were heading. Goals were set to ensure we were all on the same page and knew the next steps moving forward.

Next, we needed to look into leadership development to see the mistakes we had made, what went well, and what could be improved on. Developing leaders in these communities is such an important step in our process because this is how we are going to establish ongoing change.

Within the leadership development process, there were certain skills we wanted women to receive training on. This included both creative writing and learning about mind mapping. Creative writing gives people the opportunity to express themselves and learn how to develop this skill set further.

We use mind mapping as a good way to represent ideas and tasks that we want to accomplish. It is simple and easy for anyone to understand, as well a useful tool to let our leaders be able to give input on their own ideas and goals.

Amongst learning about creative writing, we also wanted to teach others the importance of CV writing (writing a resumé). Many women in these small communities were not given the knowledge to properly write a resumé to give themselves the chance to have a career, or even further their education.

Not only was resumé writing important knowledge to share with the people in these communities, it was also important to teach them about wills and why everyone should have one set in place. Giving this knowledge is all part of the positive impact we want to make. Mentoring and coaching women in these communities and teaching them important life skills was what we wanted to focus on next.

Yovone Cook, the Community Enabling Officer Colchester Borough Council, had this to say about the impact of the Advisory Group: I have sat on the advisory group for the Uhuru Ambassadors, set up by AFIUK, who are a group of women from different communities and faiths across Colchester. They are a voice for women and girls in the community and help to ensure that their needs are understood a signpost for women and girls who may need some extra support.

The signposting aspect of the group has been very beneficial as I have been contacted by one ambassador who needed help access help for her son who has mental health problems. I was able to put her in touch with the right people to help.

Being on the advisory group and working with the women has allowed the council access to their many different communities with Colchester, which has been especially important during the current pandemic. Without this collaboration getting vital information out into these communities would have been much harder.

"Basically, I see myself as a maker of things who knows how to support other makers of things. At the end of the day, I am just committed to helping put good stories out into the world in whatever role is appropriate and needed for that particular project."
– Mark Kassen

Reflective Questions

What are your core values?

What are the gaps that you seek to solve and why do they need to be addressed?

Identify the knowledge gaps within your team.

What skill set do you need as the leader?

Describe how you will evidence the impact of your project.

Chapter 6

Challenges and Opportunities

*"Whenever there is a challenge, there is also an opportunity to face it,
to demonstrate and develop our will and determination."*
– Dalai Lama

Every organisation has its ups and downs. At some point, a balance needs to be found to get everything working smoothly, and everyone working together properly. Our focus was making a difference in people's lives and their communities. Challenges we knew would come and go, but what we had as a whole, was what kept everything in motion. The opportunities we could create for communities was life-changing, so we needed to find a way to make what once was an idea a successful reality.

Challenges

As with any organisation or company, there are always challenges that arise along the way. Whether you are experienced or not, there will most likely be snags that will have you questioning whether you made the right decision. Our organisation had challenges due to the fact that we were a group of diverse people from different communities, and many of us spoke different languages. As with any challenge, we had to learn to overcome ours and get back on the right path.

Some of our challenges when getting our organisation started had to do with our volunteers. At first, we had trouble retaining volunteers long term. There were several reasons for this, including a busy personal life, a lack of understanding, or just being unable to fully immerse themselves into the project. While we understood why some volunteers could not be permanent, it was difficult at first finding the right people that would assist us in the way we needed.

Another challenge that arose with volunteers was how flexible they were, and the fact that some volunteers were not able to complete a project or be helpful with other volunteers within the organisation. We noticed that some volunteers did not want to share the work load, and instead found reasons not to give knowledge to new volunteers, or help in any way.

While this was obviously not the case with all volunteers, I did have some trouble finding the perfect team at first, because many people would seem to be 100% focused and ready to work as a group, but then their work efforts would slowly decrease. It was just something we had to work through along the way.

Similar to some volunteers lacking in a real work ethic, we also had a few volunteers who had signed up and showed interest, but never actually ended up showing up. This was frustrating because, when it comes to volunteers, we know ahead of time how many people we need to assist us with a certain project. If a volunteer confirms attendance, but does not actually attend, then we are then short-staffed, and the project may no longer be successful. When it comes to running a successful organisation, we need reliable staff that will not say one thing and then fall back on it. Not having enough volunteers can either make or break a project, so this was quite a challenge for us at times.

We also had a challenge matching our volunteers and staff with a project that suited them. Many of our staff had knowledge in different areas, so our goal was to match them with a project that they had enough experience or expertise in.

We wanted to be able to empower volunteers and enable them to find their own aspirations and move on to other positive changes in their life in the future. Even if a volunteer lacked experience, we wanted to assure them that they would gain experience and confidence throughout their journey, and that it would make an impact on their lives.

Our group is made up of diverse people who have different priorities and needs, so we needed to find a way to work around that, and make sure we focused on everyone's needs individually, and not just as a whole. Not one situation is completely alike, which made it challenging at times as we needed to focus on several tasks at once.

As stated before, our organisation included many people from diverse communities, and with different interests; however, we still noticed the formation of some cliques. This was mainly due to similarities within groups of volunteers and staff, which caused them to join together, and not come together with the full group. This was a huge challenge for us as we wanted our team to be completely united and work together as one to accomplish a common goal.

Another challenge came from the fact that our volunteers and staff had lives outside the organisation. While this was completely understandable, it did make it difficult to arrange who would be doing certain projects as everyone's schedules varied drastically. Many people had families that needed to be taken care of, which made it difficult for them to always attend certain meetings or projects.

It did take some time to get everyone's schedules set in place so that we could run smoothly as an organisation. Even still, schedules change, and it is not always guaranteed that someone will be able to commit to a project. We have learned through time to have a plan B, or even C set in place, just to avoid any issues ongoing.

Lastly, a major challenge for all of us, volunteers included, was the language barriers. Since we were a large group of such diverse people with different cultural backgrounds, who lived in different communities, it was not always a simple task to communicate with one another. We needed to find tools that everyone could use, such as communication apps that would change languages if need be.

We knew that everyone needed to come together and find a way to properly interact with one another to make this organisation truly successful. Just because it seemed as though we were all from different worlds at times, we knew we had a common goal. We just needed to work through these challenges and learn to overcome them!

"It's through curiosity and looking at opportunities in new ways that we've always mapped our path."
— Michael Dell

Opportunities

Once our organisation found a way to overcome all the challenges that were at hand, we could finally focus on the opportunities that each and every one of us had. We created this wonderful group to make an impact, and change people's lives, so we knew that if we made this our number one priority, we could really make a difference.

First and foremost, we had a huge opportunity to create a women's project that would provide a safe and empowering space for women. This was a huge focus for us because we knew that there were so many women in communities that needed assistance but did not know where to go to get that help.

Women in various communities had struggled for years, and we knew that there was a need for a group where women of all ages could get together and communicate to reach a common goal. We wanted a safe space so that no one felt hesitant to share their story with the group. A trusting environment was crucial if we wanted to enable the discussion of sensitive topics. If we could succeed at this, we knew we were on the right track.

Another opportunity we wanted to focus on was our plan to link communities to professionals. There are other organisations that we wanted to work with so that we could make more of an impact on the communities we wanted to help. We wanted to build a relationship with these professionals and charitable organisations, so that trust and mutual understanding could slowly be built, which would in turn create a more widespread group of people wanting to make a difference.

When it came to our volunteers, we also wanted to offer training opportunities, so that they could increase their knowledge and skills. Our main focus was on the people who wanted to make a difference in their own lives and communities. We wanted to give others knowledge so they could improve their lives, and eventually the lives of others around them.

Not only was increasing their knowledge important but teaching them important life skills was also a necessity, as we didn't just want to create a temporary fix; we wanted to change lives.

We did not only deem it important to create opportunities for the communities we serve, we also felt our Community Ambassadors should have the same opportunities. We wanted them to gain knowledge and experience by attending conferences and festivals so that they could gain confidence to start paying it forward and helping others. We also wanted to give Ambassadors the opportunity to promote their work so that they could each feel like they had made an impact on our organisation.

While these opportunities may have had their own challenges, we were not going to give up on this venture under any circumstances. We knew there were too many opportunities for people, and our organisation, to back down and not continue. We knew this was going to be worth the effort made.

"To see an opportunity, we must be open to all thoughts."
– Catherine Pulsifer

What Worked Well

Upon creating our organisation, there were many ideas that ended up working well, and there were some that were not as successful. I believe, as a whole, our group came together and learned how to communicate with one another properly to make changes in people's lives and communities.

When it came to the people within our organisation, it was clear that we all worked well together and had a bond that could not be broken no matter the circumstance. While we may have been quite different in our own ways, we had diverse strengths, positive energy, and were passionate about making a difference.

Not only did we see our team working together and communicating, we also gave witness to them empowering one another and the communities they were from. It was a wonderful experience to see people from different backgrounds focusing on a common goal.

From the inception of projects, the teams are involved in co-creating and co-production, which strengthens the connections with one another, as well as with the community. The outcomes are enormous and life-changing, because the group reaches more unchartered territories working together than individually.

Our women have several opportunities to build both formal and informal links within the organisation, their families, and their communities. Before coming together, they were just one person, one individual, which made it difficult to really make changes in their lives as they just did not have the contacts to do so.

Women working within this organisation have the ability to communicate with other organisations, or professionals who are there to assist if assistance is needed. This creates safety and opportunities for women everywhere. Not only can women within our organisation receive assistance and knowledge, they can also be a soft influence, and can be influential in educating and nurturing young people around them.

"The secret of getting ahead is getting started."
— Mark Twain

Ways to Motivate the Team

Within an organisation, there are several ways to optimize the levels of motivation in your staff or team. We wanted to motivate the team, including the Community Ambassadors and volunteers, so that they would want to make a difference in people's lives and their communities.

We decided to use something called the Learnt Lessons Forum. This was an opportunity for teams to share negative and positive learnt lessons of the project. They could discuss what worked well, and what could be improved. This was prudent information when it came to a new project, as we discovered the right steps to take.

Multi-agencies, local authorities and funders were also invited to celebrate the achievements of Community Ambassadors. On one of these occasions, the Community Ambassadors were awarded by the Mayor of Colchester, Cllr. Nick Cope, a Community Recognition Award for making a positive impact within their communities during the lockdown pandemic. Communities were able to give testimonials of their experiences, which would give us an idea of what we did well, and what we could improve on.

Another way we found to motivate the team was to give them several social platform options. We chose to use WhatsApp, and this gave the group an opportunity to communicate with one another without a language barrier, and share their emotions, vision, and values. This helped create more of a motivation as connections were made while working with the team.

We determined that the group was more motivated if the life coaches and project managers explored other creative ways of inspiring, giving feedback, and accessing funding to retain and match volunteers, Community Ambassadors and staff with their expertise, passion and choice of project team. This way, they would know what the project entailed and would feel like they could make more of an impact.

Our organisation is always actively seeking ways to offer training and support, which can be linked to qualifications or offered as evidence of experience to support women in career building, if that is what they intend to do. This motivates the group because they can succeed in their own future goals and make a better life for themselves.

We believe it is incredibly important to give our volunteers and Community Ambassadors both positive and knowledgeable experience while working with us. We want our staff to feel motivated to make a difference in people's lives.

Not everything can be accomplished within a day, and we knew that this was something long term, which would take time. Motivating our staff was the start of it all as it set the wheels in motion and gave a reason for people to keep moving forward.

*"Rachel has summarised the key elements of the ways
in which communities can help themselves. But this is more than just
a manual, it is a vision and a philosophy to help people to reach
their full potential and find their voice. It helps professionals
to understand culturally competent practice and will help everyone
to value the strengths in all our communities."*
– Sharon Rodie, Suffolk and North East Essex Integrated Care System

Reflective Questions

What is the importance of volunteers, and how can you retain them?

What do you have in place to support and motivate your team?

What are the communications channels in place, and how effectively do you use them?

What would a team building retreat day look like?

Do you exercise round table decision making?

Chapter 7

Collaboration with Other Agencies

"Never become so much of an expert that you stop gaining expertise. View life as a continuous learning experience."
– Denis Waitley

Jacqui Gitau, Co-Founder of African Families in the UK, speaks of how her journey began:

My Vision for Setting up AFiUK

For all the years when I was raising my children in this culture, a culture different from the one I was raised in, I kept looking for familiar markers, familiar reference points that I could lean on or attach to, both for myself and my children.

I came to UK in November 2001 when my eldest daughter was 17 months old, and suddenly I had to realise that, unless I was vigilant in how I clothed her, she could freeze to death. My mother never had to think of thermal vests and fur lined boots for me, but suddenly these were essential clothing for my baby in a new cold land.

I didn't have a mother, aunts, or older sisters on hand to ask questions, and even though I regularly wrote letters back to Kenya (yes airmail!) and occasionally spoke on the phone to my mother and my sisters, they could *not provide me with advice and support on the practical aspect of parentings. It was way too different.*

I quickly needed to get aunts, mothers and sisters here. I also quickly realised that my daughter needed these networks as well, otherwise she would grow up without the concept of a large extended family – a concept which is crucial to my identity as an African who gets my sense of self and identity in belonging to a community of intertwined families.

One of the first models I tried to recreate, to have my own network, was to pool our time with four other friends and form Mama Cooperative. A group of five women from Kenya, Zimbabwe and South Africa; we looked after each other's children one day of the week and worked/studied for four days. In this way we were able to provide an aunt, cousins for our children in a home with similar culture, food, and parenting style, while we were able to work/study for four days.

We did this for four years until our children were in full-time school, and then disbanded the group.

I had retrained, from my career as an office manager, to working in the Early Years Sector within a children's centre. It was while in this job that I realised that I needed to support many more families to create safe networks for them and their children.

AFiUK was born because, in my family support work, I saw how children were suffering or at risk of significant physical, emotional and/or psychological harm from parents' practices. With (African) and other newly migrant families, a significant factor that harmed the children was a result of parental ignorance of the law and what services existed to support them in their parenting role.

Having come from societies that did not have any social welfare, nor state intervention in family life, many migrant families do not ask for help, either information or practical help.

Trying to support themselves financially and even extending the support to extended families back in-home countries, many parents work long hours and are therefore not able to be on hand to parent their children.

Some parents were subject to immigration policies that meant they and their children lived in poverty, but as they were from a society where you make do with what you have, many families lived on about £30.00 per week. I saw how the children in these families were living a very different childhood from those of the other British children.

"You can have everything that you want in life
if you just help enough people get what they want."
— Zig Ziglar

Rachel Walton, Co-Founder of African Families in the UK, speaks of her journey:

I met my white British husband in 1997 in the UK. We had a long distant relationship for 10 years and then got married in 2007. We have a son who is a Third Culture child. In 2008, I started working with a charity organisation called TACMEP (Tendring And Colchester Minority Ethnic Partnership) and due to funding issues, it was taken up as a programme by a Community Voluntary Service.

To continue my burning desire to establish a Community Hub in Colchester for diversity needs which could reflect the good work that TACMEP had begun, I joined up with Jacqui Gitau, my childhood friend from Kenya and now living in Oxford, to establish African Families in the UK (AFiUK) which was born in 2015.

By creating AFiUK, Jacqui and I were seeking to create a space to bring parents together, to provide them with training and the right information in a timely way before any children were harmed emotionally. AFiUK compounds the voice of migrant families to advocate for both children and families that need that type of support. We also offer consultation, expert knowledge, and cultural awareness workshops to professionals and practitioners from the Local Authority and other family support agencies.

* * *

Mayor Cllr. Theresa Higgins Launches African Families in the UK (CIC) and involved AFIUK in Commonwealth Day (Mayor of Colchester for the year 2015-2016)

My name is Cllr. Theresa Higgins and I was Colchester Mayor 2015. I was invited by Rachel Walton to attend the African Families in the UK (CIC) launch in Colchester, Essex on 3rd October 2015 via the Mayor's Secretary. Rachel had put in a request detailing the event and what was expected of the Mayor.

I believe we had met previously at another event. My interest in AFiUK comes from the fact that I lived in Nigeria as a child. My paternal grandfather Frank Bourke worked in the tin mines in Bornu Province and my father Desmond Bourke was an agricultural officer in Sokoto province. I enjoyed meeting all the participants, and it was an honour to give out the certificates.

As Deputy Mayor I had attended the Commonwealth Flag Raising Day in March 2015. It consisted of reading an affirmation from the Commonwealth Secretary General outside the Town Hall, and then the Commonwealth Flag was flown from the Town Hall. I felt that more could be made of this day, so I had the idea of inviting people from Commonwealth countries to set up stands in the Moot Hall to share their culture.

The event coincided with Fairtrade week. As Colchester has Fairtrade status, which it has to renew on a regular basis, I was able to combine the two events for Commonwealth Day 2016.

There was a free Fairtrade breakfast on offer from 8am, the affirmation was read at 10 am, then the food, fashion, artefacts and information of 53 different countries were on display from 10am to 12 noon. It proved to be an enjoyable event by all those present, despite being held on a week day.

Cllr Julie Young, Deputy Leader of Colchester Council, speaks of her collaboration with African Families in the UK(CIC):

(Mayor of Colchester for the year 2016-2017)

I accepted an invitation to the launch of African Families in the UK on the 3rd of October 2015, and this was the first occasion on which I met Rachel Walton. She made an immediate impact on me. I found her aspiration to get more focus on African families compelling, and noted all that I learned from Rachel and the advocates there. I was the Deputy Mayor at the time, and saw in Rachel someone I could positively work with. Since that initial meeting we have been involved in lots of various meetings and gatherings; Rachel pops up often in the life of Colchester.

During my Mayoral year I was adamant that I wanted to throw the doors of the Town Hall open and engage with a wider cohort of people, and especially people who do not generally get involved in the civic life of the Borough. This was particularly the primary aim with the prestigious annual Oyster Feast, and I wanted as wide a group of people involved as possible. Rachel Walton was duly invited as she is an important voice in the Borough, representing African Families in the UK. She brings her unique energy to any occasion she is involved in.

Commonwealth Day is marked by each Mayor raising the Commonwealth Flag, but during my Mayoral year I wanted to build on the good work of my predecessor and make something more of the occasion. African Families in the UK was a natural choice, and Rachel was a great help in pulling arrangements together to make this what I believe to be the most successful Commonwealth Day we have ever celebrated in Colchester.

We had a day-long events programme and involved local schools, who learned about the Commonwealth by engaging in a range of activities. We had dance, music costumes and great fun. Rachel played a starring role in

Statements from Other Agencies

Sally Shaw MBE, Director, Firstsite

Rachel Walton has been a huge influence on all of the critical projects which are helping Firstsite achieve some success for the first time in its history since opening in 2011.

Rachel's insight into the community at large, and in particular the African community in the UK, is sensitive and rigorous, and she is very happy to share this insight to enable the whole of society to move forward together to find new solutions. In particular Rachel planted the seed for two significant programmes at Firstsite:

Holiday Fun was initiated at Firstsite because of Rachel's generosity in sharing insight into the plight of many families in the area living below the poverty line. Rachel has inspired an entire programme that has now provided over 5000 meals in the community and is in turn now inspiring other globally significant brands to follow suit.

Simultaneously, Rachel identified institutional biases within Firstsite which shed light on how new cultural forms and collaborations are critical for us to implement if we are to find new languages of exchange. This positive influencing has instigated the Arts Council Collection programme which, through Firstsite, enables a broad cross section of our local communities to directly explore and curate works from the Arts Council England National collection. The first such exhibition was Super Black, which has achieved national attention and acclaim.

I will be forever grateful to Rachel for her generosity, positivity, and open heart. She is the best possible kind of friend and colleague.

Professor Atul K Shah, City University

Rachel is a huge catalyst for change and inclusion in Colchester. She has been always ready to volunteer and share her contacts and promote the work of Firstsite. As a Curator of a special Super Black Exhibition funded by the Arts Council, Rachel played a significant role in involving the local community and selecting art that was special for them. She is always ready to help those who are less fortunate than her.

* * *

Community360

The CEO of C360, Tracy Rudling has been Rachel Walton's mentor and she has helped her in her professional development. She has provided guidance as well as connected her with networks like One Colchester Delivery Board and the Independent Advisory Group. She has helped with exploring funding streams for AFiUK and identifying tools/resources. She has made a great impact in AFiUK:

Community Ambassadors, Rachel Walton (AFiUK) and Alison Morris (Community360) have collaborated on community project work for over a decade. This collaboration has included workshops, events and idea sharing.

One of the most recent examples of this shared working approach was a set of workshops for women under a project funded by the Office of Police, Fire and Crime Commissioners (OPFCC).

In 2019, the OPFCC had commissioned this piece of work after collaboration between C360 and local BAME groups had highlighted issues of concern.

The work targeted three main areas and supported the local BAME community to raise awareness and put into place practical tools to counteract problems. These issues were:

- *Domestic Violence*
- *Safeguarding*
- *Hate Crime*

Workshops and training were specifically tailored to each citizen's cultural experience and background in order that the material be more readily absorbed and understood.

In particular, two workshops set out to raise awareness of domestic violence and to understand the experiences of women from a wide range of heritages in the local area. C360 commissioned a professional counsellor, Diane Kilgour, to run the workshops. In order to culturally curate the sessions to suit the women, the course was designed with consultation from Rachel Walton of AFiUK.

Diane and Rachel worked together to create a two-day course on the theme of women's assertiveness, which was used as a central platform to introduce the topic of domestic abuse. Women discussed how their needs were met in the home and public sphere, and women learned from each other that they had similar experiences around expressing their needs and getting them met. It was established that every woman had the following matters of contention:

- *They had difficulty expressing their needs, in both the home and public sphere*
- *They often didn't feel positively about expressing needs and had difficulty in articulating them*
- *Their needs were subordinate to others*
- *There were multiple barriers and fear in expressing their needs*

The starting point, that acknowledgement and allowance of needs is healthy and that expressing those needs to others is normal, was underpinned by a series of tools which could be used by the women in the family home and wider society if they chose to and felt confident enough to do so.

The course was effective, and the women felt relief, particularly knowing that the difficulties in expressing their needs was shared by all in the room, and that it was ok to feel the same way about it.

The course, which was terminated by the advent of COVID-19 and difficulties with social interaction, was going to include exhibiting a set of rights as a prelude to the women learning about their rights under UK law.

The collaboration between C360, AFiUK and a professional counsellor engendered a remarkable piece of work which encouraged women to look at their rights, make healthy changes in their relationships to others, and develop awareness of their needs.

The partnering of AFiUK and Community360 using a symbiotic way of working, avoiding competition in a crowded professional field, has led unfailingly to the outstanding support of vulnerable others at a local level, and unquestionable advances in community development work.

* * *

Colchester Borough Council (collaboration work with African Families in the UK)

Yovone Cook, Community Enabling Officer, Communities, Colchester Borough Council:

I work for Colchester Borough Council as a Community Enabling Officer, with a thematic lead on BAME groups. Collaboration work with AFiUK has been essential to my role, and has contributed to both of us helping residents in Colchester.

I have worked together with AFiUK to obtain a small grant for the Bangladeshi Women's Association Essex. This joint application has enabled the group to get a community allotment, two sessions with Together We Grow to help them plan the allotment, and various tools, seeds shed etc.

During the pandemic, working together with the BOAZ project, which is run by Elizabeth Alake, we were able to assist residents who were unable to access cultural food with the mainline 'Food Banks', through Essex Community Foundation, providing a grant for two weekly food bags during a nine-week 'Adopt A Neighbour' project.

Furthermore, through the 'Adopt A Neighbour' project we were able to develop a very person –centered way approach relevant to the needs of each person. This included extensive virtual outreaches and statutory partnerships to ensure the families were accessing specialist culturally appropriate services.

"I will be a hummingbird, I will do the best I can."
– Professor Wangari Maathai
Nobel Laureate/Founder Green Belt Movement

Alex Klokkaris – Personal Development Consultant and owner of Changing Lifecourse Training and Coaching:

Rachel Walton is doubtless ahead of her time in her inspirational and compassionate work, engaging and empowering individuals and groups to find their unique voice and reach for the next level of their unfolding potential.

As a long-term collaborator and supporter of Rachel's work from the very beginning, I have watched with amazement as Rachel and her team, in a relatively short period of time, have gone from strength to strength, engaging and mobilising communities for social justice, development and enrichment. Ongoing challenges were magnanimously embraced as learning experiences, in turn strengthening and widening an ever-expanding scope to reach out, address imbalances and initiate positive and real change in the community.

The impact of AFiUK's work over the years has shone light on the blind spots in our 21st century communities, reaching widely into pockets of diverse groups and individuals that have slipped through the net of mainstream support.

There is no place for exploitation and neglect in our 21st century post-pandemic world. Rachel Walton is a perfect example of how each of us can make a difference in enabling a healthy rebalancing and empowerment of our communities. Rachel and her collaborators have woven their magic through a new type of leadership, which is about empowerment and passing the baton of personal power in effecting a fairer society and positive change.

Delivering the Coaching and Mentoring programme for the Community Ambassadors left me inspired in each session, by the sheer enthusiasm and levels of engagement from the attendee Ambassadors, seeing the potential of each one as a beacon of light in their own right.

Rachel's insightful and inclusive approach shows what is possible with the right compassionate leadership, which empowers and sheds light on our blind spots. Shining the light into corners of darkness, through a strategic community-centred approach, is the new way forward to embrace our power and our potential, and Rachel has been a shining example of that.

* * *

Diverse Networking Genevieve Yusuf, Author of *Jajaja Books:*

I met Rachel Walton in my capacity as an author, as I would attend many events as a story teller, for multicultural day and Black History month at First Site.

We discovered that we both have a similar vision and work ethic and, when lockdown began, I started to teach the youth members of AFiUK about writing, starting with a journalism workshop.

68

This proved very popular, and we gathered enough material for our own newspaper, The Lock Down Times, where we would interview various talented people from Colchester, over Zoom. This taught the students many journalistic techniques, such as which relevant questions to ask, how to record information, proofreading and editing.

The lessons then evolved to include an artistic element, where we would concentrate on a linguistic theme, such a sociolinguistics, poetry, rap, or tongues twisters, and we would incorporate art afterwards, with Shermain Philip. This lesson lasted an hour and a half, and all the students have displayed great levels of concentration.

Our final piece of work was centred around how to write our own stories and create characters alongside it.

A student, Nathaniel, who can appear fairly shy/reserved, really came into his own with his story. We covered book blurbs, introductions that draw you in, book titles, crescendos and plot twists. He created a fairy tale style story, where a prince had been sent on a mission to prove himself to his father. Along the way he met a pirate enemy who he later discovered to be his cousin!

I felt incredibly proud of the way Nathaniel tackled this work. He spoke with confidence, and showed exceptional linguistic skills. I really feel like he has grown in confidence over the six months I have been teaching him.

The students have always turned up without fail, and I believe they have shown a lot of maturity, respect and diligence over this very tough time. They have listened and participated beautifully, and I have noticed many different skills and talents in each and every one of them.

* * *

Jeniffer Karina – Author of *Marriage that Lasts*

I met Rachel Walton in Hawaii, where we were both participants for Advance Leadership Training with the Haggai Institute. Additionally, I was privileged to invite Rachel to join me as my guest on a weekend coaching training by IPEC in London, UK. I have continued mentoring and coaching Rachel, and have supported her to focus on her vision.

* * *

BAME Organisations Partnership

Dr Muzvare of Girls Empowerment Initiative and Rachel Walton met in 2017 in an interfaith conference in Colchester and agreed to form one voice for women in Essex. On 19 January 2018, the Partnership of BAME Women and Girls' Voluntary Organisations was born and 10 BAME organisations met to sign a Memorandum of Understanding and formalise our networking, sharing of good practices, joint project proposals writing and identify common programmes to support each other.

This consortium of 10 BAME women and girls' organisations has been working together since then whilst strengthening their capacities to be responsive to many complex challenges of women and girls are facing. It has been a great pillar for AFiUK.

* * *

Business Networking International (BNI) – Rachel Walton's membership has proved fruitful and influential:

I was intentional in finding a diverse networking group that would help structure our organisation and give me a high level of energy and engagement to get our organisation to the next level. I found a local BNI chapter. BNI is a referral marketing organisation. The members became my marketing and salespeople; they all refer to me as the one and only Chapter's Charitable organisation because BNI has a philosophy of Givers Gain.

BNI has a training model that includes several online training webinars, videos, seminars etc. This business education and training is invaluable as it got me to learn, develop my skills and has helped me transform my both professional and personal life. I have gotten an opportunity to grow our organisation and build relationships with like-minded people who are quality business professionals in their area of operations. BNI is a great pillar for AFiUK.

"In network marketing, the whole point is not to sell a product but to build a network, an army of people who are all representing that same product or service to share with others."
– Robert Kiyosaki, The Business of the 21st Century

Reflective Questions

Reflect on your journey and write in your journal those lived experiences.

What are the differences and similarities of partnership and collaboration?

What are the benefits of collaboration and partnership?

How would your collaboration and partnership look like?

What are the benefits of professional networking?

Chapter 8

Way Forward

"We keep moving forward, opening new doors, and doing new things because we're curious, and curiosity keeps leading us down new paths."
– Walt Disney

In this complex and dynamic environment, AFiUK is committed to co-creating projects with the community to maximize our impact.

We believe that, as an anabolic energy leadership organisation, we need to find new innovative ways of fully engaging the GenZ population who would add value to our young people. Our goal is to continue working with the younger generations so that the path of change can continue to happen, and be a positive one.

Our GenZ groups are the new generation with the tools to make an impact on the world around them. It is important that we find the best way to work along with them in making a difference and showing others the right path to take in life.

Furthermore, we would like to work with men to develop Men Ambassadors, who in turn will reach out to people they know in their own communities. We want to create a resource to help boys and men of all ages in the same way that the Ambassador women have made an impact.

Community Ambassadors – GenZ

With our GenZ Community Ambassadors, we want to ensure that we are tuned into what they are focused on, and what changes they see for their future, and the people around them. They are driven by a purpose to make a difference, and they have taken it upon themselves to be stewards of this world, and in a sense, they are already leaders in their own right. Because of this, it is a huge focus for our organisation to see what the younger generations are saying, as they are the future of our world.

Furthermore, since our organisation is a charitable organisation, we are called upon to work in collaboration with GenZ charities to build stronger communities. There are many other charitable organisations who have common goals with us, and we find it important to communicate with those other charities to make a bigger impact on these communities, and the world.

The GenZ charity Community Ambassadors we have recruited are well educated think tanks who are well versed with the digital world. They are up to date with new technology and ways of communication, which can greatly help our organisation reach out to people of all ages, especially those younger generations. GenZ is a positive generation, and their desire is to make the world a better world, with their focus being on social change. They have greatly helped AFiUK in creating a more inclusive society through youth engagement.

"You don't have to have it all figured out to move forward.
Just take the next step."
– Anonymous

Men Ambassadors Project – Lawrence Walker Chairman of Black History Month in collaboration with African Families in the UK

Just as women have a better understanding of the issues of other women, men have the same or a similar understanding of the issue that most men are facing in everyday life. Men are often not as good in coming forward and asking for help with their personal issues.

We often find that men will either ignore casual suggestions to seek advice or support, feeling that they can manage on their own, or may find themselves in a situation that may be overwhelming. Men Ambassadors are needed to support other men in a way that others may find difficult, such as starting a conversation with a man about serious issues, such as mental health.

This has been the reasoning behind the launch of Prevention of Suicide Amongst Black Men. The project started as a pilot to make more men literate of the issues around suicide, and to encourage more black men to start a conversation about and to create a greater awareness of mental health issues of black men.

Volunteer numbers have grown rapidly; with more men joining the campaign with each virtual video session from week to week. The programme talks about the issues that are the onset of stress, depression, and the factors that contribute to poor mental health. We are encouraging each other to be on the lookout for the subtle changes in behaviour that may be signs of depression or reasons for concern.

We encourage our volunteers to start a conversation, and let them know that they are not alone and that there is always someone here to listen. The programme allows each to express their own personal views and concerns around these issues, and how they might affect themselves and others. Our programme is committed to stopping men from dying too young.

Men Community Ambassadors can always make a big difference, and help men live happier, healthier, longer lives by getting others to talk about men's health issues – by hosting events, talking to the media or giving talks ourselves.

As a Male Community Ambassador, you'll be embarking on an empowering and fulfilling experience that will not only change others' lives, but yours as well.

> *The reason I'm so open about this is because I want to help those who are going through the same problems and fighting similar demons. People wouldn't think twice about approaching the subject of, say, a broken leg with someone and it should be no different with a mental health issue."*
> **– Margo Arnold**

As a Male Community Ambassador, I have learned that one of the primary issues of stress, depression and mental health issues for black men is racism and inequality. Early intervention is needed to help our young people to have a better understanding of the overwhelming impact of racism, inequality and the racist behaviour that black men encounter in their daily lives.

Introducing a programme of understanding and combating racism and racist behaviour in schools is a fundamental step toward eliminating some of the elements of stress and depression and the rates of suicide amongst black men.

Our next significant step is to start enlisting an army of GenZ Men Ambassadors who are positive influencers who will work with schools.

"Don't dwell on what went wrong. Instead, focus on what to do next. Spend your energies on moving forward toward finding the answer."
– Denis Waitley

The AFiUK leaders are dedicated to providing a conducive environment, and the right local opportunities. Their goal is to nurture, coach and mentor the future leader that resides within each person, to empower and connect them to networks and teams to flourish in their area of calling.

An example of this has been the community-based organisations which are continuing to flourish with a team of Community Ambassadors who have emerged from this very process. They are actively providing advocacy and supporting families in accessing specialist culturally appropriate services.

As an example, to show this process, we have a case study to give you the best idea of the concept we are referring to.

Case Study

Jemal has a passion to bridge the gap for children with special needs within the ethnic communities, both locally and nationally. Her objectives have been to bring awareness, offer parental support, and facilitate an after-school club. Her aim is to accomplish this through emotional support, creating an information arena, sharing personal experience and skills, as well as navigating systems and referral routes coupled with online resources.

When we started working with Jemal, her main obstacles were time management, having too much on her plate, lack of manpower to assist in the completion of a Community Interest Company registration, website building, and lack of enough training to build her confidence in what she wanted to accomplish.

We worked together to identify her goals, both personal and organisational. This helped her to start prioritising everything according to importance and urgency.

As we worked together, Jemal was able to evaluate the amount of responsibility she had undertaken in the organisation. She started seeing the need to delegate responsibility to other community leaders, volunteers and fellow Community Ambassadors who would help her organisation grow.

Having done an assertive course organised by AFIUK, Jemal had the confidence to speak to the other community leaders and Community Ambassadors, recruit volunteers and delegate responsibility rather than continue taking responsibility for everything. We also looked at ways she could outsource help in building and completing her website. We were able to identify people around her she could approach and ask for help.

We looked at how working with a to do list would help manage her time well. We set small daily, weekly, and monthly goals to help meet the desired personal and organisational goals. She also attended a course on goal setting, which has added more tools to her skills.

Having a desire to support parents, Jemal was willing to learn more on how to do presentations in various settings regarding special needs. This encouraged Jemal to enrol in a Level 3 Education A training organised by AFUIK. She gained skills on how to do training through power point presentations on different topics.

She also attended a course on Mental Health First Aid, and through the session we supported Jemal to put together and prepare some training on mental health and how it affects young people, which she then presented to AFiUK'S Youth Club. She is planning to use the same skills to educate the parents on topics to do with special needs.

Through the coaching sessions, Jemal was able to look at her strengths and also appreciate the need to refer to others for help or support when necessary. Having been exposed to networking with other organisations, Jemal has managed to work in collaboration with others, and has benefitted from the support offered, as well as having contacts to whom she can refer clients needing more expertise. She also attended a resilience building course that equipped her to support the community effectively, especially during this COVID-19 season.

Jemal has completed working on her website, and she has a better organisational structure, good experience in working with people in the community, and has managed to apply for funding with Community Fund which has been approved to help support children with special needs.

"Moving forward is making things happen."
– Anonymous

Importance of Coaching in Supporting the Ambassadors

Judy Babu (AFiUK's outsourced coach and counsellor) Statements:

Sharing is caring. One of the most valuable advantages of coaching the ambassadors is the opportunity to share ideas, concerns, goals, and also to celebrate successes and learn from challenges. Coaching for ambassadors has helped many individuals establish their desired goals and take action towards achieving those goals.

Alongside side my coaching, the use of a traditional approach of sending individuals to organised trainings by AFiUK – for example, the assertiveness, and building resilience courses – has helped manage issues even more effectively. This kind of training brings an added advantage because each person is able to certify what they already know, learn more from the training, and develop the motivation to put it into practice without hesitation. Coaching has helped individuals to learn new strategies for communicating, which has improved confidence, especially when dealing with or serving people in the community.

How Coaching has Evolved through this Uhuru Project (Ambassador Programme)

As a coach, learning while coaching has become the greatest tool for me. Interacting with the ambassadors and exploring their strengths and weaknesses has opened my eyes to see some of my strengths, and how to apply myself to share my experience and knowledge with them.

The opportunity has also helped me identify my weaknesses, and the gaps in my life that needed growth and development. I have also seen the need for my own continued personal development, which keeps me afloat at all times, because knowledge never gets out of date.

Seeing me invest in my own training to be an effective coach has encouraged the ambassadors to invest themselves in training too. This has helped a lot, especially in catch up sessions where we have explored what

79

has been learnt, and how to effectively use the training they have received in their work or organisations.

Sharing my skills and experiences has developed me as a person because I have become like a book that I can always come back to as a reference point. This has also helped increase my desire to work with my coach from AFiUK for effectiveness in what I do. I have had an opportunity to learn from experts through training and supervision, which has improved in my dealings with the ambassadors and has helped me become more accountable and responsible in all that I do.

"Every job is a self-portrait of the person who does it.
Autograph your work with excellence."
– Dr. George C Fraser

Reflective Questions

What is the importance of mentoring and coaching?

What is the importance of case studies?

What are the roles of men in the family?

What does it mean to be a black man or boy in your locality?

Explore ways of engaging men and boys to participate in gender equality issues.

Chapter 9

Testimonials

Testimonials from Ambassadors

Testimonial from Grace Bedding

Greetings Rachel,

Just to start, I have learned quite a few things over the period of time I have been with AFiUK UK. I have had the privilege to study a lot and gain information that has been of great help for me as a person. Who deals with people on a personal level? I have been able to learn the right way to safeguard our children, and have learned about the mental health of children and young people.

I have also learned about the importance of being assertive as a woman in my own right, building resilience in these unprecedented times, and also being a mentor and a coach to other people. During my time with AFiUK I came across some remarkable people, who impacted me with their own flavour and style.

Friendships are built, and I am delighted to tap into the wealth of knowledge they have to offer over the course of our time spent together. Working as part of a team and how to be successful as a leader. And where you plan and execute own goals. Also, how to deal with people on more professional level. Seeing the best in people rather than not allowing them to be productive.

Everyone I met left a great impression on me, we have come to build a good relationship where we are able to encourage and empower each other.

I want to take this opportunity to thank Rachel for the great work you are doing in the community. I pray that God will grant you the grace to do more and the strength for the future.

Kind regards,
Grace Bedding

Ambassador Testimonial by Yetunde Odebiyi

My name is Yetunde (Mother Returns) Odebiyi.

I am a Scottish Nigerian based in Braintree, as well as a mother, teacher, author, nutritionist, social entrepreneur and a Community Ambassador. I was introduced to AFiUK in January 2018.

I accompanied Christine, a friend of mine, to a meeting hosted by AFiUK. I was supporting her charity, the Shepherdess. I met other like-minded ladies, including Rachel of AFiUK and Dr Muzvare of Girls' Empowerment Network.

I heard the stories of others as I shared my own story. We were encouraged to share our stories. I noticed that a lot of activities were in place for the girls separately, and also jointly for both girls and boys.

I noticed a gap in the services for our boys and young men. My passion had always been to have an organisation that preserved and maintained the African Cultural Heritage. Rachel asked if we had a registered organisation, and my response was in the negative.

Rachel advised that we look into getting an organisation registered. She offered to mentor and support us in achieving this. Rachel pointed us in the direction of Community360 for further support.

On the day of that first meeting in January 2018, a women's group was formed – the BME Women & Girls Partnership, and I was nominated the group

Admin. I came away from that meeting with lots of ideas, seeing the deep strength of women.

By May 2018, with the support of Caroline at Community 360 and that of Rachel of AFiUK, we were able to register our own CIC- Isedale Wa CIC (Our Heritage). To be able to complete the registration in my own with AFiUK support meant I was able to give myself a pat on the back and also be able to support others.

Since 2018, our organisation has been mentored and coached by AFiUK. I have attended meetings and lots of trainings to get our organisation ready for the community. AFiUK has continued to keep all Ambassadors including myself positively engaged, with course during the lockdown.

Courses I have attended with AFiUK are:

- Mental Health
- Resilience Building
- MHFA
- Safeguarding
- Assertiveness
- Goal Setting
- Plus, more

Rachel and AFiUK encouraged and supported our organisation to have a presence at all community events locally in Braintree and also in Colchester.

With the support of AFiUK, we have been able to apply for and obtain funding to carry our projects in our community.

Throughout the lockdown, and courtesy of AFiUK, our organisation was represented in all the meetings held by various government organisations and stakeholders to discuss how the BAME community could be supported.

This would not have happened without our journey with Rachel and AFiUK.

Rachel also recommended me to apply for the mentorship programme of the School of Social Entrepreneurship this year (2020). I was so elated to have gotten a place on this mentorship programme, which starts in October of this year.

My journey, my organisation's journey, has been a great experience. The support is priceless. Being an Ambassador of AFiUK has provided a great mentoring opportunity. We have met with Mayors, Councillors, and even with the High Sheriff of Essex.

We have a voice representing our community and making a difference.

Thank you Rachel,
Thank you AFiUK

Yetunde Odebiyi
Isedale Wa CIC
Our Heritage

On a School of Social Entreprenuers (SSE) session today, I was so excited to see my mentor Rachel Walton's photo being used as part of the presentation.

Yetunde Odebiyi, Isedale Wa (CIC) Community Ambassador

Testimonial by Jemal Allabayeva– Dream the Change CIC

I met with Rachel Walton, Co-Founder of African Families in the UK (AfiUK), in autumn of 2019, and we had a discussion about the challenges I was facing as a parent of a child with special educational needs. Out of our conversation came an idea to establish a community organisation to address the challenges, and fill the existing gap and support families like mine. Subsequently a few other parents joined us, and our community interest company, Dream The Change, came into existence.

Rachel's contribution to establishment and building capacity of our organisation has been invaluable. I was appointed by AFiUK as a Community Ambassador and became a part of the Ambassador's Steering Group. AFiUK offered us a lot of training and development opportunities, and AFiUK continues equipping us with vital and necessary skills and knowledge to serve our community appropriately. The mentorship programme AFiUK offers is designed to ensure proper transfer of knowledge between professionals and Ambassadors to build future leaders.

A motivational and unique style of fast-track leadership development that has been delivered to us Ambassadors by AFiUK has been far more than I thought possible. It showed us all that there are different ways of being powerful and effective. Along with other Ambassadors, I received trainings in the following areas: Safeguarding, Level 3 Award in Education, Children's Mental Health, Building Resilience, Assertiveness Training, Goal Setting, Creativity Wake-Up, CV Writing, Autism Awareness and Community Organising.

As a trainer I was offered a brilliant opportunity by AFiUK to offer a training session and make a presentation on Covid-19: youth and mental health for the youth group of AFiUK. It was an enriching, practical experience for me. The trainings offered so generously by AFiUK have improved my skills, helped me to build confidence, and equipped me with essential skills and knowledge needed to establish our own organisation successfully.

The training manager/coach of AFiUK also provides ongoing continuous support to all Ambassadors through a coach. The coach helps us to unlock our potential to maximize our performance. Other important support I got from

AFiUK was in networking, creating useful linkages, liaising with local authorities and community organisations, and building other key social connections. It helped our organisation to mobilize resources and achieve our goals.

Networking through AFiUK helped me to develop and improve my skill set, meet prospective partners and clients, and gain access to the necessary resources that foster development of our organisation. Rachel continuously shares with me relevant funding sources, community contacts, and companies who are all now part of our work.

As an experienced founder of the community organisation, Rachel supports our organisation in our ongoing projects by providing advice and technical knowledge. I hope for our future collaboration with AFiUK, as this link has been very important in building our organisation and its capacity.

Testimonial from Damaris Japheth – AFiUK Ambassador

I joined AFiUK as a Community Ambassador Representative of my local African Community. I needed to join a networking group which was diverse, and would be able to meet the comprehensive needs of my community.

I have had extensive training as a Community Ambassador, which has given me an opportunity to make a difference in my community with the skill sets acquired. AFiUK has given me opportunities to operate independently. For example, during the Covid-19 pandemic I was able to coordinate the Smile Laptop Project, for which AFiUK bought 41 laptops to give to children who were trapped by the digital divide issue and could not do their homework since they did not have laptops.

I was also privileged to coordinate the Keep Fit project for the women, children and young people to keep my community healthy.

And most of all, I have learnt about signposting and linking my community with the various support agencies that exist. For example, mental health, social services, housing, food bank agencies were essential during this period of Covid-19 pandemic.

Meet our Ambassadors
My name is Damla Kodan

My internship with African Families in the UK is completed.

Primarily, I want to thank Dr Carlos Gigoux, Deputy Director, Centre for Migration Studies Department of Sociology, University of Essex. for providing this opportunity and of course, Rachel and Judy for being great mentors. Also, all the Ambassadors who have supported me and accepted participating in my interviews throughout my internship. It was approximately a 3 months internship and I learned a lot. The internship met all my expectations, and I hope that I was a good intern for AFIUK as well. Apart from not being able to work face-to-face depends on Coronavirus, the interviews I have conducted raised my awareness, empathy, and developed my skills in conducting interviews. I am so happy that I worked with such an organization that helps many people in their difficult times. Once again, thank you for everything, and I hope to keep supporting each other in the future as well. Keep up the good work.

Supported by

Testimonial from Cllr Susan Barker

Thank you very much for your email, and for the work that AFiUK does in Essex and across the UK. Educational events, like the Migration in Essex seminar, are a prime example of how awareness raising can help bridge the gaps between minority groups and public services, and strengthen links between communities. The design and implementation of policy, on both a local or national level, should always be well informed and carried out with a developed understanding of the complexity of our diverse communities. This is why we're pleased that Essex County Council officers have been invited and have signed up to attend.

Best wishes,
Cllr Susan Barker
Culture, Communities and Customer
Member CC

Testimonial by Rachel Walton (My Personal Testimony)

My highlight of my UK visit in 1995 was when I was taken to Madame Tussauds – what an amazing place! There I met the Queen, and other great personalities – founders of African Nations like Mzee Jomo Kenyatta, Kwame Nkuruma, Mwalimu Nyerere. The desire of my heart was to one day meet the Queen in person.

This came true in 2018, when I was invited for a reception at Buckingham Palace, in recognition of those in the commonwealth diaspora across UK who had made a notable contribution, either to their own or the wider community. The Queen is a very inspirational personality, and I am forever grateful that I had that opportunity to meet her. It transformed my life.

Endorsement from Tendring District Council for one of our Funding Proposals

Leanne Thornton – Safer Communities Manager – Tendring CSP

I fully support and endorse this funding bid; I feel that we do have a gap in services and initiatives that are provided for the BME community in Tendring. What is being proposed has worked well in Colchester, I believe, and I would really welcome community based and community focused workshops, advocacy and community engagement in the Tendring District for BME communities. I have met Rachel on a few occasions at the Tendring IAG and various community safety meetings across Tendring. Rachel and African Families in the UK are passionate about providing opportunities to BME women and their families.

Rachel is playing an active role in the CSP, and has already made inroads with other partners, both voluntary and statutory, proposing to work with other partner agencies to deliver the project.

I have no hesitation in endorsing this proposal for funding as we have nothing remotely like this in the Tendring District.

Feedback and Reports from Trainers of Ambassadors

Ambassadors give feedback from the Introduction to Coaching and Mentoring Course. The training was delivered by Alex Klokkaris – Director of Changing LifeCourse

Lawrence:

As a basketball coach for 15 years, this course was an opportunity to reaffirm changes and approaches to working with people, especially young people. The course was regenerating for me, and I had the chance to reiterate skills gathered over the years. I now have even more confidence in what I want to achieve and how, and a better idea of how to achieve it. It has been reassuring that I have been doing the right thing and constantly striving to improve. I feel better equipped to tailor my skills to different scenarios and different people; in particular, communication techniques, questioning skills and challenging assumptions and limiting beliefs.

Yetunde:

The course kept me going through a tough time. I engaged with positive thinking while also being real. The work on values was excellent, and it taught me to step and observe where people are coming from. It also reinforced to me that in my work I am not , but guiding people and empowering them to access their own solutions. It has also enabled me to question my own 'stubbornness' and be better able to put things into perspective, to take a step back and really listen to people's perspectives and other ways of doing things.

Lillian Gitau Ochieng:

I would like to thank you most sincerely for this training. I have found it very helpful. It will position me to do mentorship better than I have done in the past, using skills learnt here. I help teenage girls in Kenya to overcome some of the rampant challenges that stop them from achieving their life goals.

Edith:

The course helped me to understand that it is paramount to really look and understand the other person's values and ways of being, before we engage in work together. Thank you for the guidance on how to approach, build rapport, and communicate with others to help empower them.

Christine:

I really gained a sense of achievement in this course. I have worked with the trainer before, so this was a great refresher. The main things that I am taking away with me are that, instead of trying to solve problems for others, it is about allowing them to access their own answers. I feel I have become a better listener as a result of this course. I have learned not to take over, but to allow others to make mistakes and learn from them.

Tina:

I really enjoyed and benefited from the work we did around values and beliefs, and it is something I am working with, while paying particular attention to 'unconscious bias' and staying aware. I have been using some of the approaches we learnt on the course in my work, and even with my own children, and it has been really helpful. I am interested in a trauma-informed coaching course, and also business coaching with GPs, both of which I am looking into. My interest in coaching has really taken hold since doing this course. Thank you – I look forward to my next steps on this journey.

Amaka:

A very interesting and uplifting course. I have already been using the values exercises on myself, and have learnt a lot. I have also been able to share and use some of this in my own community. It has helped me to connect to myself better, and to provide a listening ear to children and encourage them to express themselves.

Jemal:

The course was full of insights, and each session was greatly absorbing. Thank you – lots to think about and work on. I have learnt, among other things, that you find resources inside you. Also, that sometimes you have to challenge your own limiting beliefs, dig more, reflect more and ask the right questions. I loved the really inspirational quotes from Mahatma Ghandi and Alice Walker.

Training: Building Resilience During and After Lockdown

Trainer: Sarah Jones – Emotional Support for You
Report

This training was delivered to nine AFiUK volunteers. Seven completed the course and two attended for one or two sessions.

Each attendee was asked to complete a questionnaire before, then again after, the training. The purpose was to measure the impact of the training. Five attendees completed both questionnaires.

Attendees were asked to score themselves on their level of knowledge and confidence in ten skill areas that will enable them to support community members experiencing poor mental health. This report focuses on four skills:

- Paraphrasing
- Acknowledging emotions and helping clients differentiate between emotions
- Dealing with loss and grief – how to be comfortable talking about this
- Essential resilience skills and thinking habits

The questionnaires show that all participants increased their knowledge and/or their confidence to support people who are struggling to cope with their feelings during and after lockdown.

Examples of Impact Paraphrasing

This is an important skill for volunteers, as it creates a connection with a client who has spoken about their problems and how they feel. It helps the client know they are being listened to and valued.

Overall a 50% increase in confidence in paraphrasing, with one student moving from some knowledge to having a good working knowledge and confident user of these skills to support wellbeing – an increase of 75%

Dealing with Loss and Grief – How to be Comfortable Talking About This

An overall increase of a 25% rise in knowledge and confidence, with one attendee increasing 75% from little or no knowledge to a good working knowledge, and confident user of these skills to support wellbeing.

Acknowledging Emotions and Helping Clients Differentiate Between Emotions

This helps clients to increase their resilience as they understand themselves and their emotions better.

The knowledge and confidence of the attendees rose between 25% and 75%

Essential Resilience Skills and Thinking Habits

Understanding the emotional tools that support good mental health and being able to share those with clients.

All attendees increased either their knowledge, confidence, or both, by 25% to 50%.

What attendees said about the training:

"When I'm listening (to my children) I no longer say, 'I know what you're thinking.' I ask a question and listen."

"Thank you for the lessons and the breakdown of some the emotions we usually overlook. I have gained information that will be helpful to others."

"Thank you so much for the training. I enjoyed the training, and you made it very interactive. The slides you send afterwards are very useful to reflect."

"I totally enjoyed the sessions. Very thought provoking and well delivered training."

Workshop Title: Goal Setting for Leaders (3ʳᵈ Training)

WORKSHOP TRAINING REPORT
Class Size 18 Participants
Trainer Kevin Korgba (L.E.A.D Global)

Workshop Aim & Objectives The aim of the workshop was to equip the AFiUK Ambassadors with the knowledge, skills and ability to be able to set goals and prepare action plans that would enable them and any teams they lead to achieve the set goals.

The objectives of the workshop were as follows:

- Understand what goals are
- Understand how to set achievable goals
- Learn the difference between performance goals and learning goals
- Learn how to use goal setting techniques effectively
- Become more effective leaders

Workshop Format as already stated: The workshop was delivered virtually over three days using the Zoom platform. Each session lasted 1 hour 30 minutes, allowing time for questions and answers during and after the delivery.

The content was delivered using a PowerPoint presentation, with the trainer employing the use of relevant case studies, examples from personal experiences and goal setting scenarios (both personal and organisational).

Attendee Participation and Engagement

From the start of the workshop, the participants were attentive and eager to participate. The session was designed to be as interactive as a virtual class would allow, and the participants took full advantage of that. They asked questions, responded to class activities and contributed positively to the sessions. I am pleased to report that there was no disruption (technological or participant) whatsoever over the three days.

Relevance to and Impact on Participants

Based on the feedback received from participants (during and after each session), they got a significant amount of value from the sessions, and suggested that they had learned a number of new strategies that they could include in their daily personal and organisational activities.

The participants were given take-home activities at the end of Day 1 and Day 2, which were designed to help them practice the implementation of what they had learnt during each session. A number of the submissions were very revealing in terms of personal and organisational goals set by the participants.

We discussed these activities in the following session, and it was clear that the participants had a clear understanding of what goals are, the benefits of setting goals, how to set goals using the S.M.A.R.T. test, and the processes required to achieve their goals.

Practical Application of Learning

The workshop was delivered in a very practical way so that participants learned goal setting from a more practical perspective, and not just the theory.

The practical examples provided during the workshop, as well as the class activities which encouraged participants to give their own case studies and reflect on the potential issues around achieving set goals, gave that real world perspective of goal setting.

The workshop deliberately approached goal setting from both a personal and organisational perspective. This ensured that participants would be able to apply the principles they learned to their personal lives, as well as in their capacity as leaders within an organisation.

Recommendations for Future Training

This group was very professional, teachable and eager to grow. Based on the responses to the take-home activities that were set, as well as the ongoing changes to business and social landscape globally (i.e. the new normal), I am recommending three topics that would be beneficial to the AFiUK Ambassadors as individuals and for AFiUK as an organisation to help with strategic positioning and organisational resilience:

1. Emotional Intelligence: Leading and Managing Successful Teams
2. Leading Through Crisis: Strategies for Organisational Resilience
3. Personal Development: A Key to Organisational Development

Training on CV WRITING – Julia Obasa – Scriptz Writing Services

This training was aimed at empowering the Community Ambassadors. Career progression and entrepreneurship is the DNA of Scriptz Writing Service, and they are proud that they helped the Community Ambassadors in achieving their goals and becoming leaders in their respective communities, and using their transferrable skills to build their community-based organisations.

Ambassador Programme

STRESS MANAGEMENT 4 DAY WORKSHOP

With Catherine D'Arcy-Jones

A highly skilled expert in the field of Occupational Health.

AFIUK

Every Monday from

18th January - 8th February at 4.30pm

FREE complimentary Online Workshop

Join us on Zoom - For details email Info@afiuk.org

⭐ What is stress, anxiety and depression

⭐ Signs and symptoms and how to recognise this

⭐ What is stress resilience

⭐ How to manage stress from a managers perspective

⭐ How to increase personal resilience to self manage stress

Supported by

OXFORDSHIRE COUNTY COUNCIL
www.oxfordshire.gov.uk
Working for you

Essex Community Foundation

COMMUNITY FUND

supported by
www.oxford.gov.uk
OXFORD CITY COUNCIL

Community Ambassador Programme

FINANCE ADVICE 2 DAY WORKSHOP

With Rina Hicks

AFIUK

Monday 15th February and 22nd February at 4.30pm

FREE complimentary 40 minute Online Workshop

Join us on Zoom - For details email Info@afiuk.org

- ⭐ Clarify your values and align your desires
- ⭐ Understand your money personality
- ⭐ Discover your goals through investment decisions
- ⭐ How to create additional income streams;
- ⭐ Discover different investment opportunities
- ⭐ Gain confidence when making investment decisions

Supported by

What have our Ambassadors been doing this week?

AFIUK

We had the chance to enjoy a very interesting presentation by John-Paul Toh at Utility Warehouse.

Thank you John for taking the time to show us your useful money saving presentation and also explaining the opportunity to become part of the team and earning money.

Supported by

Essex Community Foundation   COMMUNITY FUND

Flow Chart - Step by Step of Ambassador Model
Empowering Women – Setting up a Community Ambassador Group

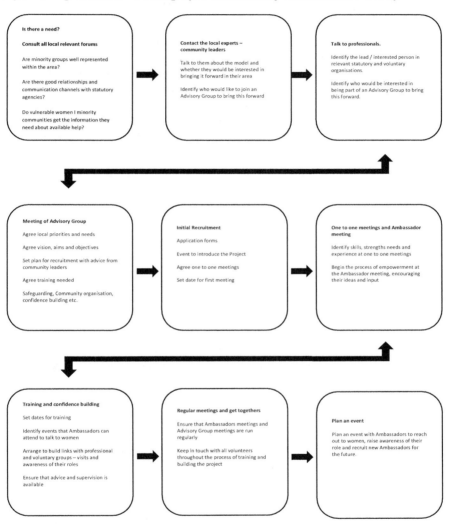

Reflective Questions

What is the importance of testimonials, and how can you use them effectively?

What is the importance of feedback, and how can it enhance learning?

What is the importance of recommendation for your funding bids?

What is the importance of a model?

Come up with a step to step of a project you are planning to implement.

Chapter 10

Through the Eyes of Kate

Kate Evans tells her story about her work in partnership with AFIUK:

Stop the Traffik is a Voluntary Organisation which works to prevent the spread of modern slavery through collaboration, information sharing and awareness raising. As the coordinator in the area, with a professional background in social work and experience of multi-agency working, I was very aware that there was a gap between the work being done by statutory and voluntary organisations working to combat this horrific crime, and community groups who are closest to the most vulnerable people, who are at risk of being victims. This makes it difficult to reach potential victims, or for them to receive the help they need.

This gap exists because of a lack of trust and understanding between minority groups and statutory organisations, particularly the police. There are many reasons for this – language and cultural barriers, fear of immigration services, a belief that institutional racism exists, a lack of knowledge about the law in the UK and what services exist to help, and a fear that people who exist in a precarious way may have their situations made worse through intervention.

This was illustrated through many stories of women who escaped domestic servitude, sexual exploitation or violence, but who were afraid of seeking help because of their immigration status. This left them in very vulnerable situations, where they could easily be exploited again, and left community members who helped them as individuals in vulnerable situations, both from a cultural perspective and through helping people in illegal situations.

There were also situations where the police identified women working in brothels, who were too afraid of the people who were controlling them to leave their situation, and "disappeared."

One of my roles was to reach out to community members and give them information. There were concerns about women and girls in minority communities who were treated as domestic servants within families, who were subject to physical and sexual assault, women and girls who were trapped in situations where they were exploited as sex workers, or in working situations where they were forced to work long hours in order to pay off "debts."

As a white British professional, it was clear that the language and cultural barriers were a huge block to reaching people to give them support and information, and that all the ways that I would normally think of to do that – posters, leaflets, awareness training, internet messaging – would not be effective for people who might be trapped in vulnerable situations.

It was also clear that the experts in this were the communities themselves. African Families in the UK (AFiUK), a community interest company, and other community organisations and churches were already working hard to support and promote their communities, and were linked to a large group of people. There were able, strong and energetic women who understood the culture and spoke the language.

AFiUK was linked to a strong network of diverse communities. It was therefore extremely important that communities themselves were empowered to take the lead in safeguarding vulnerable women and girls, supported to build trust and links with helping professional organisations, and supported to challenge issues within communities where safeguarding might be compromised.

This needed to come from communities, not from lectures by white professionals, which would be met politely but would have little impact. AFiUK was already very interested and involved with safeguarding issues, and already linked in with diverse communities, so were a natural lead agency for this work, which has been described elsewhere.

I learned a lot from AFiUK and the many strong women I met. To start with, I learned that building trust takes time, and it is important to be respectful of others' knowledge and skills. Challenge must be respectful, particularly if it is a challenge to behaviours and beliefs that are accepted as the norm within a culture.

I also learned that one way of respectful challenge is offering training from experts, with a lot of time for discussion and follow-up. This depersonalises issues, and offers explanations of UK law and culture, which are not always understood.

I also learned to avoid depersonalizing issues by using explanations of UK law and culture. I noticed throughout my experience in this that many people do not understand those types of explanations, and that can take away from the real reason we are speaking with them.

So, I learned how to properly communicate with others around me in these different communities. Throughout my time spent in these diverse communities, I realized that there is a vast range of traditions, religions, and cultures. Within these traditions and cultures, there are gaps in mutual understanding which at times has made it difficult for people throughout said communities to properly communicate and find a reason to work together.

I have learned how important it is for women and girls to find common ground so that they can help protect victims, and empower other women and girls around them to make a change.

I also noticed that certain ways of communication that are normally taken for granted in British organisational culture do not always translate well. When we had meetings with a set start time, and an agenda to cover what was being discussed, the outcomes or tasks following our meeting never worked out well.

Many women and girls in these meetings did not take well to information leaflets, but instead they communicated well face to face. We made a lot of time for talking, eating together, and listening to other women's stories, and that seemed to be of vital importance for our growing group.

While spending my time in these communities, I also noticed the differences in cultures. For example, in many Asian communities I noticed that the responsibilities of women towards their wider families were paramount, and always took precedence over everything. This made it difficult for some women to be able to be a part of our meetings and discussions, as their family was first priority.

Since there are such vast differences in cultures, I also learned it was important to be respectful of all religious festivals and traditions. Having meetings with our groups during important times throughout the year would have been considered disrespectful, so we tried to avoid conferences during times like Ramadan, for example.

Minority communities have generally had to work and struggle very hard, and women may be juggling jobs, families and study. Helping them to find opportunities to study and gain qualifications while doing voluntary work is highly valued.

It is also important to understand that offering activities and support for children is valued highly if there are clear links to future study or skills building that will help into the future. Learning to find which opportunities helped communities the most really taught me about what I should be focusing on.

Throughout my time within this organisation, I have realized that there are many women who have moved to the UK from areas where safeguarding is practically non-existent, so they had most likely had some trauma in their past. I learned that it is important to be sensitive to that. It is important to hear them out and try to get a real understanding of the experience of the victims.

Having empathy, and some form of understanding, can help greatly with their own healing process but can also help us professionals take in new information and learn from that so that we can continue to help others in the future.

Ultimately, I have learned so much while working within these communities, and I now truly have a better understanding of the world around me, and the changes that need to be made. There are so many people in small communities who need a voice, and the knowledge to know that they can make a better life for themselves, and their families.

Working with this organisation has completely opened my eyes to a world that I was not fully aware of, and has given me a lifetime of knowledge that I will take with me and teach to others.

Reflective Questions

What are your learnt lessons in working with diverse communities?

How can you develop understanding of inter-cultural competencies on issues affecting ethnic minorities?

Identify knowledge gaps you need to develop to enable you work with ethnic minorities.

References

Judge, E. (2019). Colchester Police Engagement . (email)

Barker, S. (2018). *Migration in Essex*. (email)

Thornton, L. (2017. *Tendring Bids*. (email)

Hibbert, C. (1999) George III, Penguin, London (198)

Maxwell, J. C (2001) *The 17 Indisputable Laws of Teamwork*, HarperCollins Leadership, Nashville

Schneider, B. D. *Energy Leadership*, John Wiley & Sons, Inc, Hoboken, New Jersey.

Dweck, C. *Mindset*, (2006) The New Psychology of Success, Random House, North America

Burkus, D. *Greenleaf concept*, accessed August, 2020, https://davidburkus.com/

African Families in the UK (AFiUK)CIC accessed 2020, www.afiuk.org

Walton, R. (2020) Activity submissions from my course at the Oxford Executive Leadership Programme, (Said Business School)

Kiyosaki, R, *The Business of the 21st Century* accessed 2020 https://www.youtube.com/watch?v=vikDoDp9Xr8

ACCESS (Acquiring Cultural Competence, Equalities, Successful Safeguarding) East of England, Local Government Association (ACCESS Project) 2016

Printed in Great Britain
by Amazon

80898422R00078